WHY
EVERYONE SHOULD
WAIT
TABLES FOR TWO WEEKS

Why Everyone Should Wait Tables For Two Weeks

Ian A. Gray

Master and Fool, LLC

3853 Research Park Drive, Suite 110

Ann Arbor, Michigan 48104

10 9 8 7 6 5 4 3 2 1

FIRST EDITION

Written, Edited, and Printed in the United States of America

ISBN: 0692215662

ISBN-13: 978-0692215661

DEDICATION

For the late Chef James "Gunn" Williams, who taught us
that chicken tastes like chicken, and that you can love both
Stockhausen and Faygo Red Pop and still be a fine person.

MENU

ABOUT THIS SPECIAL
COFFEE BREAK EDITION

This limited release edition of Why Everyone Should Wait Tables for Two Weeks is a preview of a longer upcoming version, and is intended as an invitation - whether you've worked in the industry or not - to share your story. In the expanded edition, we'll be including many more anecdotes, some from my personal experience as a waiter, some submitted by people like you! Learn more below.

As a result of being excerpted from a longer version, an astute reader may notice some minor discontinuity in the narrative point of view, or that not all of the characters in "The Cast" section of the book take part in "The Show". There are more scenarios and more exposition in the full-length version, which helps this make sense. There is also a more in-depth look at the history of service and class structure in the US, citing sources.

Whether you've worked in restaurants at some point or not, some parts of the book may feel downright insulting, and the tone may also seem a bit accusatory, arrogant, or presumptuous. That's probably just the jaded waiter in me talking. Part of him just won't die. But as the old saying goes, "if you're not pissing someone off, you're probably not doing it right." Whether you're pissed off or just have a story you'd like to tell, please share your thoughts at:

WhyEveryoneShouldWaitTablesForTwoWeeks.com

WHY EVERYONE SHOULD
WAIT TABLES FOR TWO WEEKS

APERITIF

I've often said that "there are two kinds of people in the world, people who believe there are two kinds of people in the world, and people who don't." But I'm going to get a little more specific here, and say, "there are two kinds of people in the world, those who HAVE waited tables, and those who haven't." One of the easiest ways to distinguish between these two kinds of people is to simply go out to dinner. While there are those remarkable few people in the world who are actually imbued with a natural sense of courtesy, grace, and dignity, these are more often acquired traits, and traits that few bother to acquire. And the absence or presence of these traits is nowhere more evident than when being served dinner by a paid stranger.

Dining in a restaurant is a fantastic tool for personality assessment, if you possess even the most meager of observational skills. On the surface, people are just procuring sustenance while engaging in conversation, but the series of interactions that take place even in a grub diner at breakfast are nuanced and revealing. We get to witness people's needs and desires and their ability to express them, and the ability of others to understand these needs and desires, and try to fulfill them. There is often also a power struggle taking place, and with a broader and deeper knowledge of what is really happening, you will come to understand that the power does not lie where one might think it does.

MY FIRST TABLE

I'll never forget the first table I ever waited on. I occasionally wonder if the diners that day remember it too. It was my third day on the job. The manager had me work as a busser and "follow" for two days to get me familiar with the place. I don't know if it was my well-pressed shirt or my quick-witted banter that caused her to believe I was ready, or if she was just mildly sadistic, but there I was. It was 1983, in a hotel restaurant that had an aging garish seventies-looking interior. It was called "The Stage Door", because the University of Michigan's Hill Auditorium was across the street, and half of the hotel and the restaurant's business came from shows that were staged there. When I say garish, I mean GARISH. It was a riot of orange and yellow arching contours against maroon carpeting, with chrome-trimmed maroon upholstered chairs. There were mirrors, track lights, and ferns everywhere. If you added an elephant, you'd have a fully decorated circus. A mirror ball, and it would have been a disco. It looked like PT Barnum and McDonald's had brainstormed together to re-brand Studio 54.

If you work in restaurants long enough, you'll probably notice that amongst all the training and management methods out there, two types are most pervasive. There's the "throw them to the wolves" method, and the "only give them two tables at once for a month" method. The former is obviously intended to weed out the rookies, but may lose the establishment a customer or two; the results on occasion are catastrophic. Most managers don't realize that the latter often has an equally negative impact on guests; take a seasoned waiter and abuse them with this level of condescension and boredom, and they'll use the extra time on their hands to figure out how to be getting drunk midshift on about the third day.

WHY WAIT

So my boss apparently was from the "throw them to the wolves" school of hospitality. A lunch rush was ramping up, and she said "Okay, we got a table for ya! We even trayed the waters for you!" Then she stepped aside to reveal a tray with ten stemmed water glasses on it. Great. My first table EVER, and it's a ten top. Was she insane? I showed no fear though, something you learn early on in foodservice. Some staffs are like wolf packs, always ready to starve out a member that shows weakness. I hefted the tray with grace; if nothing else, the fact that I was studying dance and theatre at the time gave me a little of THAT, and I proceeded confidently toward the table. So far so good. In spite of the chorus of doubtful voices in my head, I was managing to convince myself that I could pull this off.

I'm convinced that immediately after I arrived at the table and had set down the first water glass, a wormhole or some relativistic distortion of the space time continuum passed through the room, because although the next event probably took all of 500 milliseconds, my memory plays it back differently. In my memory, *The Blue Danube* plays as a tray of nine glasses is propelled in a slow-motion arc to the middle of the table, where it crashes with time-lapse deliberateness. As the glasses collide with the table, the stems break one by one, shards of glass glisten as they bounce up in slow twirling waltzes to the music, and the ice slowly loses momentum as it slides across the table in perfect radial distribution, pushing a tiny tsunami of ice cold water in front of it, which splashes over the edges of the table in a thin wall of water that arcs up slightly to ensure that it douses all the diners equally.

The next thing I know, it's back to real time in the noisy restaurant, and a table full of people out to lunch. Very

6

wet people. Some of them are already laughing it off and mopping up the water, one has leapt to her feet, and although two of them are looking mighty irritated, on the whole, they're being kind and joking about how it was a hot day anyway, and how refreshing it was or whatever. I was lucky; they were mostly actors and had all waited tables themselves. After we got things squared away at a new table, things generally went okay, mostly thanks to their good humor and patience, which - although very comforting to me - didn't change the fact that I had just introduced myself to Robert Altman by dumping water on his lap.

EARLY CAREER

After this splashy entrance into waiting tables, my career in service evolved quickly. It took a few weeks of bumbling, but I managed to nail the basic procedural stuff, and realized that my borderline attention disorder - often mistaken for a quick wit - could actually be quite an asset. While it's true that waiting tables is in fact a very complex task - requiring mental and physical stamina and agility, as well as above average social skills - the repetition of tasks means that a lot of these things become second nature quickly. And then it really comes down to *style*, and I seemed to be able to muster that.

In spite of coming from a fairly typical middle class family, I grew up in an uppity liberal college town where basic survival required being able to pepper casual conversation with references to Proust and Heidegger, and knowing that the word "espresso" doesn't have an "x" in it.

Before long, I was the "best" waiter on the staff at this first restaurant job - whatever "best" really means. In this case it mostly meant that I had acquired the robot-like skills of timing my orders, carrying big trays, and populating and vacating my short-term memory efficiently. But possessing that extra edge that makes a person *seem* like a great waiter, i.e.: the ability to "play" a table by knowing when to be witty, when to be quiet and efficient, and when to be arrogant and aloof - this made me feel like this first job was a dead-end pretty quickly. I was eager to tackle fine dining. Partly because I knew there was a lot more money in it, but probably just as much because I wanted to escape the ignorant yahoos I was waiting on, the ranch dressing and ketchup crowd.

Although I didn't know it at the time, those last references were to be the first wrong turns in a lengthy and often deeply unsatisfying career in restaurants. Why were those two points so important? We'll explore this in much detail later, but first of all, it's an unfortunate truth about life that you will find "ignorant yahoos" all the way up the affluence scale. And secondly, if you ever reach a point in life where you actually judge people's character based on whether or not they like Ranch dressing on their salad or ketchup on their steak, you really need to examine your *own* character. Or shoot yourself.

So this belief that I was destined for something better in the world of waiting tables, a belief that seemed to follow me to each new job like a seedy collection agent, was something I eventually resolved. But not before it led me to my first job in a high-end restaurant.

My first experience with fine dining was in a place that served French country cuisine - you know, Cassoulet, Coq au Vin, that sort of thing. The fact that at the time I couldn't tell a lamb shank from a lamb *chop* was no obstacle; about eighty percent of the guests couldn't either, and as a quick study I knew more than they did within a week. And the remaining twenty percent? Thanks to their arrogant and condescending nature, all I had to do was sound fascinated with their vast world experience - which was mostly comprised of a trip to France twenty years ago - and they'd love me for the opportunity I provided to make the poor working class waiter guy look like an ignorant twit.

It was at this fancy joint that I received my first lessons in condiment classism. At one of the first staff meetings I attended, the cockiest waiter on the staff reaffirmed with the owner - much to everyone's delight - that not only would there never be a bottle of ketchup in the building, the staff actually had permission to chuckle if a guest asked for it. This was also where I learned all the skills so important to being a good fine dining waiter. Things like the detached staring off into space while opening a bottle of wine instead of looking at the task at hand, the smug air of utter disdain, and snarky comebacks to "train" the guests instead of letting them walk all over you. It's amazing how subtly obnoxious you can be if you never make a mistake and food arrives exactly at the right time, and the table is cleared silently and stealthily with impeccable timing. After a few months, I felt I was ready for "the big time", and my eagerness to take things to a new level coincided with an opportunity to move to San Francisco. I was ready.

Or so I thought.

The average person - unless they're a bloodthirsty stock broker, and they're not really "people" - will never know the utter cruelty that can exist behind the scenes in food service in general, but especially in fine dining in a major city. My introduction to this phenomenon was in a restaurant in San Francisco. A newfound friend had gotten me a shoo-in job at a pricey place that was on an old dry-docked sailing ship. The menu was based on classic Italian fare, and the place was awkwardly divided into lots of small dining rooms connected by nooks and crannies that acted as service stations for things like bread, silver, coffee, etc. I was a little nervous my first night; this was a place that operated on the "throw them to the wolves" training method I mentioned earlier. My nervousness was magnified a bit by the confusing layout, the demanding and surly clientele, and the fact that I was not only new at the restaurant, but new in *town*. But none of that compared with how the staff helped me learn the ropes of the place. It was a six-hour exercise in pointless cruelty based on intentional misdirection. If I asked where something was, a co-worker would smile and kindly explain, and then I'd find myself wondering which part of their directions I had missed, when I'd end up staring befuddled at a bread station when I had asked where coffee was, or when someone asked me to run some drinks for them, and I'd find myself waiting at a service bar for cocktails that were never to arrive, because they'd been served halfway down the "ship" at another service bar. It was on the second or third of these fool's errands that I spotted a couple of co-workers doubling over with laughter, and realized this was going to go on all evening.

After this nightmarish first shift at my new job, we of course all went out for drinks. But as I had a few genuine laughs with some of the crew about my "baptism by fire", I feigned other laughs with the more asinine staff members. Because I was also making mental notes of which of them I would target to make their life a living hell. I quickly adapted to this brash and cynical approach to work, and succeeded within a few months at taking away the job of one of the headwaiters who had exhibited the most genuine mean-spiritedness that first night. And as I got to know the city, I found much better jobs, sometimes with truly wonderful people at places that were run with a genuine passion for great food and a positive dining experience, but just as often in that jaded sort of environment of my first job in the city.

This laid the groundwork for my attitude toward almost every job that followed. There are a lot of stories to share, some funny, some not, and we'll get to them later. But first, let's explore with a more objective point of view the many dynamics that help create the ups and downs of dining out.

SOME HISTORY

The next time you find your waitperson furrowing their brow as you bark orders or make meticulously detailed demands of them, ponder this: you have very little in the way of legitimate grounds to do so. How dare I make this brash, judgmental statement? You may be thinking to yourself "oh, you're just saying that out of sympathy because of your own miserable waiting career!" But the fact is, I'm basing the claim on historical record, and the historical record suggests you're probably both from the same social class, and in some cases, the server may in fact be from a "higher" social class than the guest. Are you already bristling a little at this assertion? Unless your name is Rothschild or Mountbatten-Windsor, give it up. Let me explain.

Something that is rarely discussed about the restaurant business in America is that by and large, it's a relatively new invention. Although you can trace the existence of public eateries of different kinds all the way back to ancient Rome and China, the restaurant as we know it didn't become common until the 19th century. While inns and lodges commonly served food prior to this, it was considered part of the business of hospitality. Otherwise, the only folks likely to have men and women in crisp uniforms serving them food were royals or affluent leaders of commerce and government, and the people serving the food were permanent staff, who often lived on site. You know all those Dickens-era stories about rich people slavering over fat juicy ham while the poor made bone soup? You may recall that Dickens never said much about taking the family out to Red Lobster on Fridays. That's because there was no such thing as a middle class that could enjoy the luxury of having food and wine brought to their table on a whim in the evening, and the next morning mow the lawn of their "estate" with a lawn mower paid for with income from their *own* service sector job. For hundreds and hundreds of years, the only people who had people serving them in any way were wealthy landowners, and the only people serving them were people who *weren't* wealthy landowners.

The French Revolution and the American Industrial Revolution can be given most of the credit for changing all that, and when it comes to most server/guest frustrations, most of the *blame* as well. If you're not already putting the picture together here, walk this through with me. After more than a millennia of human experience that was largely shaped by a precious powerful few being served by a plentiful impoverished many - in some places and times by actual *slaves*, we suddenly - in the span of less than a hundred years - switched the class structure and redistributed wealth in such a way that the role of master and servant may be entirely inverted in some cases. It's not at all uncommon these days for the person playing the role of servant to be from an "old money" family and merely paying their way through college, while the person playing "master" could be a wealthy real estate agent whose parents lived in a shack in Appalachia.

It's kind of fundamental to human nature to believe that one deserves the best, even if one doesn't. And this strange free market invention - the modern restaurant - proves this point. Surround the coarsest, most ignorant person you can find with fine linen, sparkling glassware and silver, candles, and servants in freshly-pressed uniforms, and they will quickly start playing the role of king or queen, insisting that heads must roll if their every demand is not met without question.

To maintain the illusion of this tragicomedy, a modern restaurant provides the stage, complete with the props just mentioned, and also handily provides some extras and bit players, in the form of guests and restaurant staff. The role of servant/butler is replaced by the modern waiter - an accurate replica of the original except for one important costuming detail; he's been stripped of the dignity typically worn by a butler.

Now that we've outlined some historical background, we're almost ready to tell the story.

We just need to flesh out the cast.

THE CAST

THE BOSS

I referenced on the first page of this book the danger of using the "two kinds of people in the world" framework. There is of course the old joke that "there are two kinds of people in the world: people that think there are two kinds of people in the world, and people who don't." In reality, I fall into the latter camp, but it can be a handy framework all the same. So I'm going to go out on a limb again here, and assert that there are two kinds of bosses in the world: those who know what they're doing, and those who don't.

The foodservice industry seems to have no shortage of the "those who don't" types. This is probably driven by two main factors, which have an important commonality. The two most likely reasons that someone ends up owning or managing a restaurant are either (a) They had the capital and the dream (some would argue insanity, restaurants are one of the least reliably profitable businesses to get into) to start one. Or (b) They had an interest in the foodservice industry, and actually got some kind of hospitality-related degree.

The unfortunate commonality here is that neither of these types is likely to have waited tables or worked in a kitchen, and they bring this obvious inexperience to every decision they make. There are of course exceptions; some of the greatest restaurateurs I've worked for or with came from unrelated corporate backgrounds, and chose to get very hands-on when they opened their restaurant. In the process, they embraced the essence of why everyone should wait tables for two weeks. But sadly, these are the statistical oddity. So let's explore the various ways that ignorance, arrogance, or knowledge can blend to create a restaurant experience.

Dilbert Clouseau, Your Maître d'

In case you were wondering, that's pronounced *"dil-bare"*. You may have worked for this fellow at some point. It's said that after his first strategy meeting with the *Brigade de cuisine*, he was quickly nicknamed "General Failure". It's a basic fact of restaurant life that if you work in them long enough, you'll inevitably work for some pompous numbnut who has absolutely no idea what he's doing, but somehow talked his way into managing a restaurant.

I had the pleasure of working with a perfect manifestation of this stereotype at one point, a man who honestly had to have been one of the most oblivious and inept managers in the history of fine dining management. I say "pleasure", because his arrogance and obliviousness were not only exceptionally entertaining to me and the other seasoned staff members, they also made it possible to "run one" on him incessantly. He never had a clue what cruel tricks we were gaslighting him with; he probably wrote off his disoriented evenings at work to his age and vigorous alcohol consumption.

He possessed exactly *zero* restaurant experience; he was brought in as a manager by the affluent owner of the restaurant, presumably because he was so good at *talking* about how restaurants should be run - having spent so many hours in them criticizing their shortcomings. He was an hilarious expression of Oscar Wildean debauchery, attempting highbrow wit with a wink at any opportunity, always while downing surprising quantities of Chardonnay.

In his late sixties, six foot five, with a shock of white hair, he spoke with a thick Scot-like churl even though he had moved to the states in his early twenties, and never had contact with Scotland again in the ensuing forty-some years. He had a plethora of affectations like this. He seemed to have memorized the entire *Collins Dictionary of Quotations*, so was never short on witty quips like "Champagne for my real friends, real pain for my sham friends". He also did silly things like betting you he could finish the New York Times crossword in twenty minutes, not realizing that you were as crafty as him and knew he had already completed it at home that day, and then grabbed a fresh paper on the way to work.

Never to be seen without a glass of wine in hand, it was hard to tell if his welcoming blather at the door - with which he routinely informed guests that they could have a table in the packed dining room in mere moments, in spite of the clear impossibility of this - was alcohol-fueled or ignorance-fueled. No matter, we still had a blast with his drinking problem. He expected a glass of wine to await him on his arrival, and we would always have it ready. We would then spend much of the evening refilling and moving it a couple of feet periodically, for the cruel pleasure of watching him look panicked and confused as he tried to locate it again. Other tricks included things like using made-up words for common restaurant objects and tasks to see if he would adopt them to appear knowledgeable about the business. But this fellow, in all his arrogant and ill-informed proselytizing at staff meetings, said one thing that was very true, and very useful. He said, "fine dining is like the theatre", pronouncing that last word "thee-uh-tuh", with just the right amount of pretension, of course.

Although the fact was that it probably only *seemed* like a theatre to him, because he was much more drunken spectator than participant, the remark was the basis of an important truth. The concept of "theatre" is essential to a great restaurant experience. It needs to be balanced with quality food, quality service, genuine hospitality, and a sense of pragmatism, but it is definitely an important component. And a theatre needs a cast. And direction.

THE MEAT CLEAVER WIELDING MANIAC

A sense of drama or downright insanity definitely isn't *required* to run a good restaurant, but it can certainly make the process more interesting. This type of owner - in spite of the distorted impression you may have if you watch "Reality TV" - is much less common than one would think. I personally only worked for a few people like this. Usually, it's more of a detriment than a benefit to the establishment, but sometimes it's a sign of genuine genius at work. One of the most brilliant people I've ever worked for was this type; it's rumored that he literally DID chase people around with a meat cleaver and yell at them, but he backed up his insanity with an astounding level of insight about food and hospitality. He patented a pasta making machine early in his career (long before Americans even knew there *was* such a thing as "fresh pasta"), and opened a Sushi restaurant over a decade before the trend became more popular in the 1980's. You could probably base an entire book on this fellow, so we've included some of his stories in the anecdotes at the end of the book, and on the website. In any case, regardless of his genius, he was a maniac. But people love slasher movies, and this fetish seems to carry over into restaurant management.

MISTER HOBART

This is the saddest man on Earth. Did you know that over 60 percent of career restaurant managers are white males around the age of forty, divorced, and make less than forty thousand a year? No wonder they also work an average of sixty hours a week - their life would be meaningless otherwise. These are the relentlessly cheerful fellows that you see looking haggard (and maybe bloated from an occupational alcohol problem) at Olive Garden. They're also the only people on the planet that call restaurant guests "covers" and dishwashers the "Hobart Man" with no sense of irony. They have taken the reason that everyone should wait tables for two weeks to a tragic terminal state.

STAFF

BRANDON & TIFFANY

Brandon and Tiffany are the waitpeople who walk up to your table and say "Hi! I'm Brandon! And I'll be your server tonight!" as if their mere arrival at the table isn't an adequate announcement that they're there to serve you. They then launch into an annoying and overly-scripted delivery of the evening's specials, asking if they can start you off with a Kiwi Mango Marguerita garnished with Pomegranate to wash down your Rellenos Buffalo Wings with Ranch Dip, tee-em. Throughout dinner, they'll try to grab your plate without asking - usually while you're in the middle of slicing into your entree - but later ask "can I take that for ya?" after you've put the empty plate on the floor simply to get it out of your way, because you haven't seen them for twenty-seven minutes. Every time they appear at the table, they'll say "Is everything GREAT tonight?" They often pronounce espresso "expresso".

WHY WAIT

Sebastian. Or Sergio. Or whatever.

This is that arrogant jerk who walks up to your table and sounds like a BBC radio announcer mumbling the stock market report as he informs you of the specials in a pretentious and droning sing song. You never really get a good look at his eyes, because he has his nose tilted so high that it obscures the view. In spite of never really losing his cool, he snorts and sighs a lot when you make any special requests. Although he may perform all the routine tasks very professionally, he always seems to be sweating slightly, and looks really tired. That's because he's also a raging alcoholic, whose only real concern this evening is making it smoothly through another shift, collecting his tips, and hitting the bar after work so he can erase all memories of waiting on you and do this all again tomorrow.

H. Houdini

We'd love to describe this waiter for you, but no one has seen him since he brought the menus and water. No one is quite sure, but it is assumed the "H" stands for "Haven't seen him".

Velcro Marx

This is the lost Marx brother; the one that ended up waiting tables. He clings to the table with such abandon that you begin to wonder at some point if he's planning to come home with you, but he is in fact merely a frustrated standup comic whose last gig was the table before yours. The tomato on his shirt is not sauce he spilled; it's from actual tomatoes thrown at him by the last table to make him go away.

GUESTS

DICK

Dick is unhappy. He's fifty-three years old, but has never had a good experience in a restaurant. He's probably an alcoholic, but his massive credit card wealth and pedantic knowledge of food and wine mask this. He's often a little red in the face and sweaty, but knows what a Full Windsor is, and somehow manages to tie one with his sausage-like fingers. He rolls his eyes and snorts a lot, but never complains directly. This way, he can justify his 11% tip at the end of the evening. If you work in food service, the only thing about Dick that may bring you pleasure is the fact that he will die of a massive coronary within seven years, or get sober in three and be a swell guy for the rest of his life to make up for lost time.

MR. AND MS. CAMPBELL

The Campbells are a stingy clan. Their main concern is not usually whether the food or service is exceptional, but whether the *price* is exceptional. They prefer a soup & salad combo, but on occasion they like to splurge. After watching the local newspaper circulars for several months, they will eventually find a place that for one reason or another is offering two-for-one specials on dinner, and finally decide it's time for a night out. When they arrive at the restaurant, they'll try to customize the clearly defined discount in some way, and whether they're successful or not, they'll order no beverages, no extra courses, and skip dessert. And along the way, ask for incessant water and breadbasket refills. You can easily spot them at the end of the meal, they're the table with all the people with calculators in hand, repeatedly passing the guest check around and pointing at items, shaking their heads.

CHIP AND MINNIE ATKINS

In case you're wondering, Chip got his name by carrying one on his shoulder most of his dining life. He really doesn't know much about food or wine, doesn't have much class, and has no palate whatsoever. But what he lacks in those areas, he makes up for with an abundance of insecurity and a high income from his work in real estate. His bristly nature with the server and endless criticism of the food that he knows nothing about are a smokescreen for his secret discomfort. He'd rather be on the golf course, and have a simple steak and fries at the country club afterwards. All of this obsessive and carefully cloaked unease of his enables him to ignore the fact that his wife orders everything in halves, on the side, and low, un, or de whenever she can. Breakfast? An egg white omelet, with lowfat milk and half decaf, half regular coffee, with dry toast. Lunch? Soup (does that have any dairy in it?) and salad (dressing on the side please) and a diet coke. Dinner? For God's sake, just roll out the damn birdfeeder and a box of Chardonnay. She's already eaten her 950 calories for the day, and has some DRINKING to do, dammit.

PARKER TANZER-ROTHSCHILD

Parker knows more about wine than probably anyone on the planet, including himself. He knows what all those letters on Italian wine bottles stand for, and he uses words like "garrigue" and "terroir" comfortably. Never mind that this comfort comes from the fact that he knows that no-one else knows what the hell he's talking about half the time, he really does know what the words mean, and he'll use them. In fact, he'll use them so much that at some point it will become impossible to enjoy the stuff, because instead of being a simple accompaniment to some nice food, it will become little more than a vehicle for Parker's exposition as he reveals his vast encyclopedic knowledge of wine, often veering off into discussions of noble rot and popes. Parker also seems to often be a bit red in the face, and his obsession with wine makes it difficult to tell if he attends 5 daytime wine tastings a week because he's genuinely passionate about wine, or just has a drinking problem.

THE SHOW

We've made a couple of references to the idea that foodservice is a bit like theatre, but here's the real deal: the main way in which it's like the theatre is that there's so much suspension of disbelief going on. It's hard for us to believe that this miniscule and poorly executed entree we've just been served costs $34.95. Maybe it's so expensive because it *is* a prop, crafted by union theatre workers. We can't believe that the person that's serving us still has a job, after screwing up in about a half dozen ways since we sat down, and still treating us in a condescending and defensive fashion. We can't believe we're missing a perfectly good night of FREE television and a cool beer to sit cringing every time we sip what passes for a Manhattan at this place. The waiter can't believe what a bunch of Pinot Grigio swilling yahoos he's waiting on. We can't believe the people at the next table won't shut their kid up for one goddamn minute. No one can believe pretty much anything that's happening, if they're honest with themselves. But we sit and enjoy the show anyway.

So. We've outlined the cast, and painted the storyline in broad strokes, but let's move this show from pitch to script, and do a slow read-through.

ACT I

It's Friday. You've had a long week. You've decided to meet some friends at a trendy new local restaurant around 5:30pm to treat yourself to a pleasant evening. Upon your arrival, the young host makes up for their lack of finer social skills by at least being smiley. You get seated, and it seems like a bit of a wait before the server appears, mostly because you're kind of anxious to kick back with a glass of wine and unwind. When the waiter finally arrives, you jokingly say something like "You guys must be really busy, huh?" even though the restaurant is nearly empty. You're really just kidding around; you're aware that there 'are a million reasons the waiter might have been slower showing up than you like. Their smiling reply seems a little forced, probably because your attempted irony has been tried by thousands of guests before you in the same situation, but they ask if you'd like something while you wait.

You ask if they have a nice Chablis. The waiter smirks and smugly chortles a bit, then suggests a Chardonnay. He returns in a slightly more timely fashion with your wine, just as the first of your friends arrives. The waiter hovers, hoping to get a drink order from your friend. You and your friend ignore the hovering waiter as you greet each other. He eventually shows his impatience as your friend futzes with the wine list, providing their commentary on the quality of the list, asking if you should get a nice bottle, and then finally ordering a glass of cheap Merlot. The waiter returns quickly with the wine again, and even though you and your friend are waiting for four other people, you ask about specials and specific items on the menu. This process of ordering drinks as your friends arrive one at a time continues, and your group ends up asking about specials several more times before you've all arrived.

Especially after your friends like Dick, Chip, the Campbells, and Parker have shown up, the waiter has probably made exactly three times as many trips to the table as should be necessary for the number of guests present, and he's beginning to show a little impatience. You probably don't realize it, but some seasoned waitpeople call Friday and Saturday "Amateur Night", because people who know how to dine do it every night of the week, but about ninety percent of the customers on weekends *only* eat out on weekends, and it shows.

ACT II

Finally your party is settled in. Then the cross-examination begins. "What's YOUR favorite?" someone asks the waiter. Chip and Minnie ask some dumb questions about why the lamb is served medium rare and not slow-roasted like the lamb they had in France that spring, not realizing they're chops and not shanks. At some point Dick asks "what's your name, young man?" and the waiter replies – with a bit of a snark - "It's Sebastian, what's *YOURS*?" Dick then references some obscure piece of information that is intended to make Sebastian look ignorant, but Sebastian surprises everyone by knowing more about the topic than Dick, which Sebastian gladly demonstrates with a subdued arrogant glee. Parker comes to Dick's rescue though, and completely skewers Sebastian over his ignorance of the wine list, an ignorance that Sebastian can do little to remedy, because although his boss Dilbert Clouseau gladly cracks open hundred dollar bottles to impress friends on a regular basis, he considers wine training a waste of time that eats profits and wastes perfectly good wine. Perfectly good wine, apparently, for HIM to taste test nightly.

As the evening hums along, you don't realize that Sebastian is waiting on a half dozen other tables; a brooding married couple, a couple of obnoxious MBA's trying to outclass each other and prove how gay they aren't because they don't have dates on a Friday, and some group that has never eaten anywhere fancier than Applebee's, and is celebrating a birthday. As he gets busier, maybe he makes a mistake or two. Dick claims he makes a mistake he *didn't* make. In the ensuing exchange, no one ends up happy; Sebastian resentfully offers to fix the problem, but Dick then passive-aggressively says, "no it's fine I'll just eat it". He'll later use this as one of many excuses to notch points off the tip, when he makes a big show of slipping Sebastian his Amex Black card and saying loudly "Don't take anyone else's money. I got this." Dick doesn't realize that Sebastian is going to include the gratuity, and present a check that still has a blank line for the tip, so when Dick thinks he's leaving a 10% tip as punishment, Sebastian will be laughing in the kitchen about the 28% tip.

ACT III

It's hard to tell if Sebastian starts serving from the wrong side and neglecting to clear dishes out of ignorance of basic service, or out of mild contempt for your group. But the group doesn't mind so much, they're getting a good buzz going. Even Dick has relaxed a bit, a sure sign that in about an hour his mood will plummet back into gruff impatience, when the group is having lots of after-dinner drinks and debating the fine points of the desserts they will never order, and all Dick wants is to go home and pour another scotch. All in all though, no major catastrophes have occurred. But nothing really exceptional has happened either. As the evening winds down and Sebastian and your friends no longer have dinner between them as a point of contention, civility returns, maybe even - at least for the moment - an earnest friendliness. It's like you've all been through something together, and can finally relax and let your guard down.

CURTAIN

Yes, this was a rather unremarkable show. But frankly, most of our lives are; they only *seem* interesting when we're starring in them. Just be thankful we didn't do an actual *cinéma vérité*, play-by-play version. What we *did* include in this little script were some key dramatic points that we'll get back to after we talk a little bit about the Life and Death of a Waiter. Life, as they say, imitates art, and both have their critics. And understanding one person's fairly typical performance on the stage of service will lend a lot of nuance to the critique we'll serve up later.

THE LIFE AND DEATH OF A WAITER

There's probably a sweet spot in the arc of every server's career. You don't want them waiting on you when they're a total novice; they'll forget things, always be trying to steal your plate while you're still eating, and ask constantly if you need something instead of just recognizing it by visual cues. This seems to be a perpetual state for some waitpeople; these types should take the title of this book to heart in a different way, give their two-week's notice NOW, and find some other line of work. You also probably don't want the waiter who has gotten *too* comfortable with the routine at their first restaurant job; they'll tend to treat you like an uninvited guest in their home (which you are, in a way; see "How to Be a Customer" later in these pages) and either act arrogant and indifferent, or get too chummy like they own the place or something.

You also don't want the waitperson who has worked long enough to master every aspect of the job exactly as thoroughly as they've learned to detest their seemingly dead-end, mindless existence. They'll present so well at the table with their easy smile and meticulously scripted style that you'd never in a million years believe the things they may be saying about you or doing to your food when you piss them off. That last bit - your gift for pissing off a waiter - is why we included the "How to Be a Customer" section, and in fact a big part of the reason for this book's existence.

This middle phase is where a lot of professional waitpeople freeze in their development. They've mastered the job but ultimately think they're above it. They have plans for something like returning to school, or getting a "real" job, as if *their* job isn't real. That's another grand mistake in foodservice; it can actually be a rewarding and respectable career choice, but our culture is embedded

43

with the notion that the job is only a temporary solution. Because, you know - we ALL have the God-given right to life, liberty, and the pursuit of happiness, and we're all going to be millionaires some day.

The trap of foodservice is two-fold. The first element of the trap is the money. A smart, motivated person in a major city can find foodservice jobs that net them $40,000 a year, with a four-day work week and considerable flexibility with those four days. Few other types of unskilled labor can generate better income, without requiring that you put on a hard hat and carry a lunch pail to work Monday through Saturday.

The other element of this trap is rarely talked about, but is way more pervasive than one might imagine. I would bet good money that if you dine out tonight, your server is either hung over, slightly buzzed, or maybe even just plain drunk. Don't bother betting against me though; there are statistics to support this assertion. A 2010 study presented by the National Institute of Health found that 80% of men and 64% of women working in foodservice exhibited "hazardous alcohol consumption patterns". But some of us don't need scientific studies to tell us this; having worked in the business for a couple of decades, I assure you that the respondents to this survey were either under-reporting slightly, or didn't respond at all. Because they were out having a drink!

That's a pretty wicked double-edged sword we've just outlined above, especially when you factor in the self-esteem issues we described prior to that. I thought I was really clever and insightful the day it occurred to me that one of the main reasons I drank my brains out every night after work was partly to forget how much I detested what I had just done, but also to ensure that the job would be challenging again the next day when I tried to perform it with a brain-splitting headache, nausea, and cold sweats. *Wouldn't want to get too bored with the job*, you know; where *else* would I make this kind of money and be able to drink on the job? But before long, I met other career waitpeople who would have the same epiphany, quite often as we were enjoying a Bloody Mary or Mimosa with a pre-shift brunch. I never knew until I waited tables that you could drink with a meal at two in the afternoon and call it "brunch".

So where is this "sweet spot" we mentioned at the top? It's hard to predict. I've met some waitpeople who managed to find some magical balance for years, never getting too bitter, never getting too consumed by the after-shift drinking, somehow nailing a calculated detachment in spite of the fact that in their heart, they detested the job. And then there are people who actually BELONG in the job, and LOVE it. I don't mean to give the impression that *no-one* in foodservice is happy. I personally believe it's quite a respectable career choice, and there are plenty of people who have an admirable passion for it.

But for the rest of us, there is definitely a sweet spot. Mine was fairly early on, and lasted only a few years. The rest was an extended personal nightmare that eventually led to a greater awareness of how to be human. Let's call it...

THE DEATH OF A WAITER

I really, really loved the first few years that I worked in restaurants. Constantly learning new things and meeting new people, accepting the often surprising challenges presented by providing hospitality to sometimes oblivious or cruel guests. And as a very social person, I made tons of personal connections. But after a few years, I ran into my first glass ceiling. You see, in many restaurants, there is a fairly rigid (if unspoken) policy of not promoting within. An employee may work at the place for several years, and know the ins and outs of the business as well or better than even the owner, but the owner remains the owner no matter how oblivious they may be, and new management is usually hired in at entry level. A smart or appropriately humble employee knows to play the role they've been assigned, or even to brown-nose the new management to protect their job.

I was neither smart nor appropriately humble about things in my early career. My first experience with the phenomenon of threatening a manager's authority had a rather hilarious outcome. I had been working in the restaurant in which I had spilled ten glasses of water on Robert Altman's table for about two years when a new manager arrived on the scene. He was short and portly, and looked somehow like a seventies porn star interpretation of the miscreant offspring of Hitler and Napoleon. The dictator vibe came mostly from his diminutive and angry presence; the porn star quality was suggested by his Tom Selleck moustache. He didn't like my confident nature and the respect my co-workers generally displayed for me, and immediately began riding me with inane commands in the middle of busy shifts, and attempts to institute trivial changes in procedure to make his presence known. After trying to stay under the radar while disregarding his general idiocy for a week or so, I got called down to the office after a hectic lunch.

He was sitting behind his disproportionately large desk as I entered his office. The effect was almost comical; he looked like an actor playing a child on an over-sized set in a comedy sketch. I'm sure I had a smirk on my face as I sat down and he began outlining the problems he had with me, and I could tell somehow that this was more than a reprimand. He finally got around to saying "and those, I'm afraid to say, are the reasons I'm going to have to let you go". I stared at him for a moment, probably still smirking, but now with some indignance, before I said, a bit contemptuously, "So. You're FIRING me?" He leaned back smugly, putting his hands up behind his head. "That's right pal", he said. Now HE let a smug little smirk creep onto his face. At that exact moment, a button popped off of the shirt his corpulent torso had been poured into, and bounced across his desk, landing in my lap. The unexpected comic relief was too much; I stood up laughing like Tom Hulce's Mozart in the film *Amadeus*, and walked slowly out of his office, pausing once at the door, just to look at him and burst out in another wave of laughter.

That laughter was of course in large part fueled by discomfort as much as it was by the serendipitous sight gag, so when I walked out of the building, I headed to a favorite nearby bar, and for the first time in my life got absolutely shitfaced at three in the afternoon. But in the process of drowning my sorrows in alcohol as I told my tale of woe several times, something else serendipitous happened. My bartender friend said "Hey, come back next Monday and put in an application. We're hiring a bartender, and I'm pretty sure I can hook you up". This pretty much ended my waiter career for a while, and launched the next phase of my service career.

The Birth of an Asshole

It's a routinely overlooked fact of life that there are few people on Earth more powerful than a bartender. In the several years that followed, I never abused this power, but - like many good bartenders - certainly enjoyed it. If you've never worked in a restaurant, you would only be vaguely aware of the sudden wizard-like power often given to a bartender, who may just the day before have been waiting tables. It's like some secret Masonic Initiation has been completed. To be fair, the job does in fact not only have a great deal of responsibility attached to it - I mean, human lives are literally in your hands - it also requires special skills to excel in the position. A really great bartender is part therapist, part chef, part waiter, and in some cases, part bouncer. Knowing how to mix the twenty common cocktails is a virtually useless set of knowledge without some of these other gifts or skills. I seemed to possess all of these skills in abundance, so the next several years of my life were shaped mainly by the bizarre schedule and distorted sense of self-importance that only the drug and alcohol fueled world of nightclubs can provide.

And in my case, another chance to hone my gift for getting fired. '

This first bartending job was in a popular live music venue. I already had some basic skills with audio engineering, and once the owner discovered this, I was suddenly doubling as sound guy. This meant I was often working in the club six days a week, putting in more hours in many cases than the owners themselves. Who, by the way, were quite the odd couple. The money behind the place came from the six-foot-two wife with blonde hair and beak nose who had received an immense payoff when her first husband was killed in a tragic construction accident. The mismanagement of the place was graciously provided by the man she quickly married after receiving the settlement, a short Irish fellow with a shock of wild white hair who parlayed the staff's ignorance of UK accents into a distorted belief that he was from Liverpool, and had been good friends with the Beatles. His mismanagement consisted mainly of spending too much money on renovating the club, and walking around holding a rattling teacup and saucer as he struggled to get his Antabuse dose on an even keel. Because of the hilarious juxtaposition of their respective appearances, the staff called them Big Bird and Papa Smurf.

This job was the second example of one of my many experiences in failing to learn the most valuable lesson that restaurant work can provide a person. The value of humility. Humility is often misunderstood as ingratiation, when in fact all it really is, is an honest perception of your place in things, and an understanding of how dependent your existence is on others. It's the ability to remain "teachable" in almost any situation, regardless of your presumed status within a hierarchy of other humans.

I didn't think much of this concept at the time though, so when Big Bird and Papa Smurf appointed their son as a manager, my problems began. The fact that the fellow had no idea what he was doing - he was about twenty five and had been an EMT for several years - was compounded by the fact that he REALLY didn't want the job, and had only been forced into it by threats of having his financial umbilical cut by Big Bird. And he was doomed in a way, because the staff knew this. The closest thing the place had to a manager at this point was me, but this was only because I was on premise over sixty hours a week, not because I had any official authority. My "position" ended the first week he was on the job, when he insisted I turn the music off when we closed. If you've worked in service, you've probably learned that an establishment gets cleaned up and closed about 80% faster if the staff can blast loud music of their choice, as opposed to futzing around in a dreary empty space with dish machines and vacuums droning, and the random noises of glassware and silver clattering and mops sloshing.

Unfortunately, Son of Big Bird didn't get this, and after a brief shouting match over New Order's "How Does it Feel" blasting through the sound system, I conceded and turned the music off. Mostly so he could hear me clearly when I said "John, you're not only a f***ing moron, you're an ***hole". When I showed up the next evening for work, I was told to head to the office. When I stepped in, Papa Smurf handed me an envelope, saying "Sorry lad!". This was when I first realized that I was ALWAYS going to have to ask the inane question "So, you're FIRING me?"

A Meteoritic Career

Please note that I said "meteoritic". It could have been a *meteoric* career, but meteors don't crash to Earth. Getting fired from the best live music venue in a small Midwestern college town should have humbled me, but it didn't. It only fanned the flame of my passion for the addictive cycle of service as self-abuse. I soon had another bartending job at a bigger, cooler club. Pretty soon I was promoted to the position I like to refer to as Dickhead Doorman. A nice restaurant has a gracious and confident maître d', a good hotel has a gracious and hospitable concierge, and a trendy nightclub has a total dick standing out front, pulling a rope aside for graft or hot chicks. At the height of my career as a Dickhead

Doorman, I thought I was invincible. Owners would ask for and implement my advice on themes and decor for the club, I was chummy with the cops in spite of the fact that I often had a half ounce of coke on my person while working (I was often the club's resident drug dealer too), and although I had learned how to fight pretty well myself as an accidental side effect of my profession, I always had a couple of huge thugs standing behind me, backing up my motormouthing with brute force.

Yes, I was invincible. For a few years. The cycle ended when I somehow managed to get hired and fired at the same club four times. Three times under one owner, the final time when new owners came in. The new owners wanted to "clean up" the staff, which in reality meant, "get rid of people they couldn't control and replace them with their own". On a slow Thursday night, they for some reason put me on as bartender on an upstairs bar that was only likely to open if business picked up quite a bit, and it wasn't. Typically, the person scheduled in that slot would be released by about 10:30 on a slow night. It was past eleven, and they still hadn't opened the bar, but I heard a rumor that two of the top bartenders had already been called down to the office and reprimanded, and told that if they shared any details about why, they'd get fired. I knew something was up when, at 11:30, they told me to open the desolate third floor bar. A few minutes later, a manager came by, and ordered a round of shots for themselves and their friends who were visiting from out of town. They insisted I do the shot with them. In spite of basically being a violation of liquor laws, this was a totally routine practice at almost any nightclub in the US that I ever worked in. They slammed their shots, left me a tip, and went back to wander the club.

WHY WAIT

A few minutes later one of the other bartenders came to the bar and said they'd cover for me for a few minutes; the boss wanted to see me. As I descended the three flights of dank nightclub stairs to the basement office, I began smoldering more and more with each step down. By the time I reached the office, I somehow managed to restrain my rage as I calmly said - before anyone else had said anything - "So. Are you FIRING me, or WHAT?" There wasn't much discussion about the topic, as you can imagine. A couple of the thugs who just hours ago were my staunch allies were instructed to escort me out of the building.

Finally, some kind of message about humility sunk in. But getting fired this way was only a catalyst. This time, I *didn't* find a cool new job immediately. And this forced me to face that the fact that staying awake until 5am, drinking a fifth of hard liquor and consuming a gram or two of coke daily, and sleeping until noon were perhaps not especially useful behaviors.

MAI TAIS, AND MY TIE

I was hilariously forced by financial necessity at this point to get a couple of crappy jobs, one at a Tiki bar, and one at a pretentious and trendy bistro called "Cars". Something about wearing a Hawaiian shirt for one half of the day, and then spending the other half of the day in a restaurant that had mannequins and car parts protruding from the wall quickly took its toll. It didn't help that the owner of the Tiki place was a raging old chicken hawk who wouldn't keep his hands off my ass, and the owner of the car-themed bistro's real expertise was in yelling at the staff in Arabic, not running a restaurant. Guess what happened next. Yup! Fired. Two times in one week. This time I practically begged for it though, so wasn't at all surprised. My personal life was a bit of a shambles, so I did the only logical thing. I got ANOTHER job in foodservice. This time, returning to the small town I grew up in, and once again as a waiter in a high-end restaurant.

I thought returning to a more sensible environment, doing a simpler job would be good for me. What I didn't factor in were a few important details. One was that although I was quite accustomed to working with several drinks in me, and having ready access to more when I wanted one, this was not exactly in the standard waiter job description. The other was that since I had basically dissolved the walls between various restaurant positions, I had a TERRIBLE sense of boundaries and absolutely zero patience for anyone who couldn't do the job as well as I could. While drinking, of course. My career as a cocky, hard drinking jerk came to end at this establishment. On an especially busy night, I had been demanding cocktails for myself from the bartender. She wouldn't make them, so I'd grab them myself when she was busy serving someone. I was still managing my tables well, but this little game became quite a distraction, and was having a terrible effect on my buzz and general mindset. It all came to a head when I was picking up a large order from the kitchen. I had no trouble loading the six dinners onto a tray and hefting it to head out to the dining room, but as I headed out of the kitchen a co-worker said something to me, and as I turned, I somehow pitched the entire order onto the floor squarely in the entrance to the kitchen. The same bartender who was refusing to make me drinks then delivered one of the best improv lines I ever heard in a decade of foodservice, which was "Could you guys drop three more pastas, two coq au vin and a shank? IAN just did."

This actually could have been a total non-event; people just have accidents like this now and then, and I had pretty much NEVER had a mishap of this sort, in spite of being half-drunk half the time. So the kitchen guys - bless their souls - whipped up the entire order again in no time. I trayed it again, hefted it again, and headed out of the kitchen again. Unbelievably, another co-worker was standing in exactly the same place as the one earlier, said something I couldn't quite hear, and with the precision of a laser-guided missile, I tossed the order onto the floor in EXACTLY the same spot. Something in me came unhinged at this point. I made some half-assed attempt at helping clean up, but then I just became enraged with myself and my existence, and started muttering "fuck this" repeatedly as I went through some zombie-like motions of turning my tables over to other staff and punching out. As I stormed out the door, I felt free; free in a way I had never felt before. Somehow, tearing off my tie and tossing it into the street was an integral part of this ritual. I headed to a nearby bar and celebrated my freedom with a bunch more cocktails, silently deriving satisfaction from the fact that the bartender wasn't arguing with me about whether or not I should be having them.

The next day I woke up wondering, of course, if I still had a job. You may think the answer here is a forgone conclusion, but in years of restaurant work I had seen plenty of people keep their jobs when much worse things had gone down. My hope was short lived though; the familiar ritual of someone handing me an envelope as I arrived for work was re-enacted once again. The bartender who had delivered the great one-liner the night before was technically my boss, and to her credit, she made the tough call of firing me, more in the hope that

I'd straighten out my drinking problems than out of malice. I would have maybe been able to stomach this humbling blow, but as she was politely letting me know I was fired, one of my suddenly-former co-workers walked up and said "Hey Ian, we found your tie in the street last night when we were leaving", and handed me the tire-tread-stained piece of silk I had so gleefully thrown into the abyss the night before. I managed a wincing, scrunch-faced "thanks" as they handed it to me.

I still have that tie today, as a reminder of the next little phase of my career, the story of which I hope will convey why I believe - as the title of this book suggests - Everyone Should Wait Tables for Two Weeks.

JUST DESSERT

Although I now look back on the demise of my waiter career with a lot of humor, it was more than a little humbling to get fired from a waiter job at the age of thirty, and it certainly put things in a new, clearer focus. Obviously, a big factor in that last of many firings was my drinking, so I quit. This alone triggered a total paradigm shift in my day-to-day life. Within just a year, I had taken a few computer-related courses, and parlayed this into a moderately successful freelance income doing website design for small businesses. As an act of redemption of sorts, one of my first clients was the restaurant that had last fired me. I did the job entirely gratis, partly to have something in my folio, but probably more to make some sort of amends with a group of people whom - when I wasn't drunk and waiting tables - I actually *liked*.

Although I was finding some success doing work completely unrelated to restaurants, I still hadn't truly snipped the umbilical cord. There were a few factors at work. One was that I couldn't help noticing how my extensive experience in serving the public gave me a notable edge over other tech-industry freelancers when pitching a job, something we'll get back to in depth later. Another was that I simply kind of missed the work! It had after all taken up much of my first decade of employment as an adult. But to be honest, the simple fact was that I needed more money than my freelance income was providing. This led to a brief resurrection of my waiting career, and a series of mini epiphanies that led to a total change in my outlook on life.

REMAINS OF THE DAZE

So on my knees, with my hands clasped in a prayerful, pleading gesture, and with a sorrowful brow and longing look in my eyes, I awkwardly kneed my way into the office of the manager who had fired me. This is not an exaggerated description for dramatic effect, I actually did this, and we both thought it was pretty damn funny. The restaurant business being what it is, I was forgiven, and hired back part time. We agreed that getting drunk was not part of my job description, and that if I dropped six dinners during the first thirty days - especially if I muttered "fuck fuck fuck" repeatedly after doing so - that I would likely be terminated. I was strangely happy to be giving this all another shot. Later that day, I bought some fresh "black and whites" and some new ties, and when I was done shopping, decided to rent a couple of movies on the way home.

This was probably one of the most significant visits to a video store I've ever made.

As I perused the aisles, I ran across the film *Remains of the Day*, based on the novel by Kazuo Ishiguro. I didn't think much of it at that moment; a Merchant Ivory film is a Merchant Ivory film, even if someone brilliant like Anthony Hopkins or Emma Thompson has a lead role. But that evening, as I watched the film, I had a mind-blowing epiphany about service. If I opened a restaurant today, I would make this movie part of the mandatory training material for the service staff.

Why? Because Anthony Hopkins' portrayal of a butler embodies the very soul of what service is about. Service is about humility, dignity, and professionalism. Although the character of Mr. Stevens may carry this to an almost self-destructive extreme, translating the *essence* of what he was doing to *any* service job will transform the experience into something almost transcendent for all involved. It's useful to note that the distinction between humiliation and humility is one of personal choice.

Although the words come from the same Latin root which means "of the earth", the evolution of the *perception* of this core meaning has led to some confusion that diminishes the almost divine nature of humility and being humble. The implication being that since humiliation is a state caused by one person maliciously highlighting another's weaknesses or flaws, that somehow being humbled or expressing humility are expressions of weakness.

Nothing could be further from the truth; it in fact takes incredible strength of character to walk through life with humility, and possession of it is often a person's greatest strength. As Golda Meir said, *"Don't be humble... you're not that great."*

A key scene in *Remains of the Day*, the one which in fact triggered my little epiphany, is when one of the arrogant and affluent men visiting the estate asks Mr. Stevens what he thinks about the epic, world-changing events being discussed, and Stevens courteously and matter-of-factly replies "It's not my place to be curious about such matters". The wealthy fellow's condescending insistence that Stevens must have *something* to say on the topic ultimately demonstrates which of the two possesses the most class and dignity.

This was when it hit me. There is no shame in humility, but plenty of humiliation will arise from shame.

RESURRECTION

So the idea that watching a Merchant Ivory film starring Anthony Hopkins could change a waiter's life may sound absurd to you. If it does, that's because you've either never waited tables, or have, but missed out on one of the most gratifying aspects of what it's all about.

Have you ever hosted a perfect event in your home? Maybe a simple dinner party, or more lavish event? By "perfect" I don't mean one of those parties where everyone gets so rip-roaring wasted that all anyone remembers is how much fun it was hugging the arresting cop naked when getting arrested on the last beer run when the jello shots ran out. No, I mean one of those evenings where it just seems everything went perfectly, and you were left with a profound sense of serenity and satisfaction. Good food, paced and presented well, good conversation, a gracious host, and a timely conclusion where everyone seems to sense it's time to leave at the right time, and leaves with contented goodbyes. These are rarer than they should be, because there's pretty much only one thing required to create them. What do you think that one thing is?

Humility.

You could argue that "no, actually it was that five hundred dollar Bordeaux that made the evening special", or zero in on some other singular characteristic that pleases you personally. But the fact is that it is really simple humility that makes an experience like this tick. At least as a *collectively* gratifying experience. Whoever is hosting exhibits it by offering their home and preparing food for others. The guests exhibit it by enjoying the food uncritically, and making it a pleasant evening with civil, interesting conversation. And perhaps graciously offering to help serve or clean up at some point, and not arguing if the host refuses. Or groaning if they accept.

When this kind of event takes place in the home of an extremely wealthy person, the process is made even easier for everyone involved, because there is service staff that is properly trained and properly compensated, an air of restraint is engendered by a lingering concern about pleasing the influential host, and the host themselves have a vested interest in maintaining their impressive reputation. This still requires a sense of humility all around, because maybe the host is so much more highly placed in society that they really ARE humbling themselves to "lesser" guests. Or maybe one of the guests is vastly more important or influential than the host. And in any case, everyone present is presumably human, so differences like this are purely contrived. Especially in the case of the service staff, who - as Anthony Hopkins' character demonstrated in *Remains of the Day* - may be the most sophisticated of everyone present. I personally have certainly seen this play out in real life, when a friend who had made fast money in the tech industry would routinely be outclassed by the service staff of friends from "old money". Often not even realizing it. In the end, modeling my behavior after the best service staff I had seen in "real" life helped shape my new style as a waiter.

MY NEW CAREER AS AN ACTOR

So the approach I used upon my humbling return to service is going to sound terribly contrived. But it worked. And it quickly became very natural feeling, and rewarding. This was not just my subjective experience of it all either. My tips - which already reliably averaged twenty percent, beating out most of my fellow staffers by three to five percentage points - rose to an average of twenty-five to twenty-eight percent*, meaning that a fair number of guests were tipping over thirty percent. This doesn't happen by accident. So what did I do?

I embodied humility.

This was largely an acting job at first, and although I stuck to the role with unerring commitment, some elements of it felt incredibly hokey in the beginning, and made me laugh almost hysterically when I had breaks, mostly because I couldn't believe the guests' acceptance of it all. When I say, "I embodied humility", the fact is that I was literally just replicating - to the best of my ability - the mannerisms and style of Anthony Hopkins' butler character in *Remains of the Day*. So there was an added layer of "meta", in that I was in fact not only acting, I was acting like an actor acting!

So what *exactly* did I do in this acting like an actor role? I literally cloned the behavior of a classic English butler, save for the accent, which I think would have taken it over the top and rendered the act the comedy you might think it would be in the first place. I intentionally adjusted my posture to stand upright, never with a hand in a pocket or casually on a hip. I made sure my shirts were immaculately white and pressed, and brought an extra each night in case of a mishap. I arrived at the table enthusiastic, courteous, and attentive, but never gregarious or overly familiar. I always began with "Hello, how is everyone this evening?" and politely asked if they would like to hear about the specials, and if so, if they'd prefer drinks first.

No matter how busy I was, I placed every item on the table with calm assuredness, and removed or replaced items with the same quiet care, bending at the hip and not over-reaching, with one hand behind me if appropriate. I didn't initiate banter, and when addressed directly, responded with raised-brow enthusiasm, but restraint that didn't stray into a realm that suggested I was an equal, or a friend. I also added some subtle touches like pouring wine in the style of an English butler, placing the end of the bottle over the glass, pausing, pouring gently, tipping the tip of the bottle back up (no "rolling") and pausing without withdrawing (rarely, if ever using a cloth to dab the bottle) and then drawing back in a straight line to repeat the process with the next guest.

I always took a step back before turning away from the table, and would utilize a subtle bow of the head or body in place of the many verbal acknowledgments a waiter might typically use. "Certainly" became the word I uttered most when a request was made, and if the request were something unreasonable or likely to be unachievable, I would say "I will certainly do my best and inform you if there is a problem".

In essence, all I did was recognize my place, which was to serve, and unerringly did my best to accommodate the desires of the guests, and do it in a dignified and professional style. This may seem like an obvious approach, but for all the reasons outlined earlier in the book, you will rarely - if ever - experience this kind of service, because both the server and the guest are almost universally inept at knowing their role and playing it with dignity. The service experience is often perceived merely as a brief contractual arrangement, with both signatories knowing fully well that in another setting, these parameters would be irrelevant.

I have to confess that in the beginning, my hearty laughter during breaks was more about shock and discomfort than humorous disdain. I couldn't believe I was humbling myself to this degree, without a sense of feeling ingratiated or humiliated. I had spent half of my adult life refining a carefully executed balance between contempt and unquestionably professional service, a method that - while it got the job done - probably left all involved a bit more cynical, and a bit less gratified. It was a method driven entirely by arrogance and cleverness played against insecurity. And here I suddenly found myself acting in the most humble fashion imaginable, and ENJOYING it.

And this is the core of *Why Everyone Should Wait Tables for Two Weeks*. It would create a more dignified, civil world. If you think the problems of foodservice are entirely the fault of those serving, I guarantee your view would change if you witnessed firsthand the shortcomings of those being served. And if you're a server who feels above your job, you really should consider embracing it properly or find a new one. Hopefully one that can instill in you the simple wisdom of living with a little humility. It's a powerful thing.

So to explore these dynamics from both points of view, let's return to that hypothetical dining scenario we presented earlier.

*Yes, some fine dining waiters are this meticulous about tracking income. And in my experience, most servers barely maintain a fifteen percent average. This was in any case an accurate figure in this instance; I was constantly comparing notes with co-workers.

CRITIQUING THE SHOW

Okay, let's go back now and review "The Show" from a few pages back, but through the cynical eyes of a snobbish critic of dining behavior. This is pretty much point-by-point.

ACT I

Your arrival at the restaurant at 5:30 - ordering a drink straight away - immediately suggests that you're either working class, or an alcoholic, or both. Most genuinely affluent people may have had wine or cocktails with lunch, and for that matter might still be drinking, but they'd be doing it on their boat. And anyone with actual class would sit tight until a companion arrived before starting to drink.

Your attempt at humor is also misplaced; why do you want to build a chummy relationship with someone you actually plan to have catering to your every whim all evening? And as already mentioned, your witticism is probably a hackneyed one. If you were actually funny, you'd have a job in comedy, and be having this first drink down at the bar where all the hip comedy people hang out in the early evening.

Now, it's the waiter's turn. His pretension when asked about Chablis embodies two problems. First of all it's, well, *pretentious*. Not to mention the fact that there are in reality some great Chablis wines; his snootiness about this is based on some outdated presumption that a person ordering Chablis is an ignoramus who thinks they're ordering the "Ernest & Julio Gallo Jug" version of Chablis.

You then reveal more bad manners and amateur diner traits when you start planning dinner before all your guests have arrived, and wasting the waiter's time. You might argue that they're called "waiters" for a reason, but a professional server might also argue that Friday and Saturday are called "Amateur Night" for a reason too.

ACT II

Often, an evening out is doomed from the beginning, and the more observant amongst us can see the clues right away. Here we have a classic turf battle between a smartass waiter and an arrogant diner to carve up the territory of who is smartest and most arrogant. The dick-waving usually centers on food or wine knowledge, and when a combatant finds themselves losing the battle *there*, they'll broaden the scope to try and talk about the country that produced the food or wine, and even push beyond that into the obscure political history of it all or something of that nature. This is a risky pursuit on both ends; chances are the server knows the specific dish being served better than the diner, but even if the diner stumbles here and then resorts to making the waiter look bad in revenge, there's a good chance that waiter is in grad school and can hold their own in that realm too. In the end though, the waiter is finally chopped down easily enough by ordering them to do something.

But that is only a battle. The war is not over yet.

Our waiter Sebastian - in spite of having taken a job that is entirely based on the concept of serving - feels put upon by simple questions like "what is your name, young man", or by any observations that he has performed his job imperfectly. And frankly, part of this has *some* legitimacy; a guest demanding the waiter's name without offering their own first IS a little rude in some way, especially since it usually is intended to imply a little "ownership", rather than a genuine intent to get to know the waiter. But Sebastian is a fool for being fazed by this. If he wants to keep his name a secret, he should have a "work name". I've known dozens of foodservice pros that do this so that they can tell how someone in a bar later knows their name, when they have no idea who the person is. And the rest of the treatment Sebastian doesn't think he deserves? It's surprising how effective detachment in the face of such things is. If a server keeps their cool (read: humility), many groups of diners will clamp down on their obnoxious cohort *themselves*, and the whole experience will elevate slightly in terms of class and civility.

ACT III

We mentioned the classic double-tip trick; this is probably WAY more prevalent than you would imagine. And the kind of subtle mangling of service details that a waiter can engage in to make your experience less pleasant can range from Sebastian's passive-aggressive sloppiness or neglect, to a server actually doing something you'd rather not know about to the food that you're putting in your mouth. In two decades of foodservice, I only witnessed this once, but the time I did made me realize it must really be going on out there, and probably in the most disgusting ways imaginable. This kind of act takes things to a really different level, and it takes a really different kind of person - a nearly sociopathic one - to stoop to this. But the version I witnessed - a bartender who would put a very personal part of his body in a drink when a customer pissed him off - occurred in a very upscale hotel restaurant.

But most of the things that go on that demonstrate all the things wrong with the diner/server relationship are subtle. And they all center on one simple concept, so we'll mention it again: humility. And oddly, the onus is not entirely upon the server to be humble, it rests equally on the served, and the intertwined actions of an entire restaurant crew, from the dishwasher to the owner. But there are often a lot of imaginary lines of battle that can make it a challenge to get all these people to work in harmony.

BATTLE LINES

I just counted, and I have worked in precisely seventeen restaurants in my life. I'm skipping the half dozen or so nightclubs I've worked in, because they didn't have kitchens. Care to guess how many of these establishments had a consistently civil relationship between kitchen and floor staff? Two. I don't have hard data to back up this next assertion, but my hunch is - based on random shop talk with other restaurant workers over the years - that I fared pretty well.

The ranting, cursing and insults through the chef window are not only fodder for comedy scenes in foodie movies and the lifeblood of reality TV programs about the industry, they are often a basic part of the job. Why? Well it probably doesn't help that this area of the kitchen is called a "line", and that most of the people working behind it are holding knives half the time. It's pretty easy, when two overworked people are standing in a sweltering enclosed space, face to face (because that's pretty much all they see through the service window), for both of them to forget they're actually on the same team, and the real "enemy" - if there must be one - is either the boss or the customer.

But this way of framing things is probably where all the problems begin. From almost every vantage point - the guest, the server, the kitchen crew, the manager, the owner - it's not hard to immediately identify potential adversaries. The line in the kitchen is an obvious one, simply because it's, well, a *line*. But without that essential ingredient I keep talking about, i.e.: humility, pretty much *any* interaction can become a confrontation, and "lines" can appear everywhere. Having managed several restaurants, I assure you (as I mentioned in "The Cast") that the manager is usually at the absolute worst possible nexus in the larger scenario. A server may be at odds with a customer, or at odds with the kitchen, or at odds with the boss, but all the confrontations are relatively fleeting, and easily forgotten by the next shift. A line cook may have a bad night because of an inept server, or the boss may be riding their tail for an evening, but likewise, these frustrations are ephemeral. But the manager? On a bad day, the manager is in the precise center of all the problems that can arise in a restaurant, and usually the solution to one problem is going to rely on creating *another* problem elsewhere. Give the customer a comp? The owner won't want to see too many of *those*. Reprimand the kitchen over a cold entree? You better be sure it wasn't the server's fault. On a day when everything is falling apart, the manager is inevitably going to be catching hell from every direction: from the customer, the staff, the owner.

I don't really have any useful suggestions for managers except "find a new line of work"; they've sort of made their own bed with their career choice. But almost all the other problems we experience in a restaurant are easily avoided, by (are you getting the hang of this yet?) exercising a little humility. In this broad context, all we mean by "humility" is knowing your role, and playing it well. In the Theatre of Food, don't be a critic, be a player.

If you don't know how to play your part, don't worry. Whether you're on the production or consumption side of the invisible lines we create, we've got you covered with some unsolicited and somewhat condescending suggestions for how to do what you do, and do it well.

HOW TO BE....

I'm not generally in the business of telling people how to be, but in the case of dining out, I'll make an exception. While there is of course the occasional miscreant who violates even these common rules of etiquette, we somehow manage to collectively get the idea that we shouldn't talk on the phone at the theatre, or hoot at the U.S. Open, or fart on the bus if we can avoid it. So why is it that no matter which end of the stick we're on when it comes to dining out, there seem to be so many people who can't grasp the simplest guidelines for civility and humility?

Well, I've actually gone to some lengths to try to answer that question already; it probably *does* have a lot to do with the class confusion that our culture makes possible, by encouraging poor people to get rich without any requirements for dignity or manners, and rich kids to work in restaurants to prove to dad that they're not thankless freeloaders.

But the fact remains that for almost every sour experience that occurs in a restaurant, the blame rests as much with the customer and the support staff as it does with the server. So here's my unsolicited advice about...

HOW TO BE A CUSTOMER

Great. Your bookshelf is packed with titles like *Kitchen Confidential* and books by Anthony Bourdain and Charlie Trotter. You program your DVR to record *Avec Eric* weekly, and can't believe Sam Sifton hasn't won a Pulitzer Prize. Your favorite websites are Urbanspoon and Zagat, and you've dined in some of the finest restaurants in the world. Surely if something goes wrong with your dining experience, it is the restaurant's fault, probably the waiter, right?

Think again.

That kind of thinking comes from the head of a person whose life is a demonstration of *The Peter Principle*, i.e.: the phenomenon of "rising to the level of one's incompetence". A person with any class (or any humility, since they often go hand in hand) knows that the real responsibility for maintaining an elevated state of interaction while dining rests just as much with the guest. You can hardly expect a struggling restaurant employee - who may have come from literally any social strata, from the hills of Tennessee to the country clubs of Connecticut - to maintain the *élan*. If you have any class yourself, you already know this stuff.

But if you're *struggling* to have class, consider taking the chip off your shoulder when you dine out. If you're not a truly knowledgeable gourmand, just relax, enjoy the food and company, and learn - if indeed that's in the offing. There's no shame in not knowing everything. I've seen more potentially pleasant evenings out decimated by pretension than I care to recall. The experience of dining out in America is particularly influenced by that thing we pointed out in the chapter "Some History" - which is the fact that as the land of equal opportunity, we have no clearly defined serving class, and haven't since the late 19th century. On the one hand, your waiter may have a PhD in Macroeconomics, and on the other hand, your guest may be an incredibly unsophisticated but affluent real estate mogul. Both will be aspiring to some imagined sense of etiquette that only exists in British novels and old-money clubs frequented only by Rockefellers and Vanderbilts. And both will likely fail miserably.

And speaking of Rockefellers and Vanderbilts, you probably aren't one. So why do you feel entitled to ignore your server for extended blocks of time when they arrive at the table? You're probably talking about last night's episode of *American Idol*, for God's sake, not the new oil field you just started drilling off the coast of Venezuela. Yes, the waiter is there to serve you. So let them!

SOME THOUGHTS ON TIPPING

If you have a problem with the idea of tipping, eat at home. Or use your immense influence - since apparently you're such an authority on wage structures and labor - to pass legislation that requires waiters to be paid the same way everyone else gets paid. And then sit tight while the tectonic shift in the industry occurs, because the kind of sharp-witted people that populate wait staffs nationwide will not do the same job for the kind of crap pay they'd likely end up with.

So deal with it. Fifteen percent is an absolute baseline. You're only demonstrating your lack of class if you tip this amount; most civilized diners tip eighteen or twenty percent. Got a problem with the service? Address it with the manager, not passive-aggressively through the elaborate demerit system that you use to legitimize your crappy tipping tendencies.

Aside from the fact that there are a million possible reasons that are beyond their control that may have caused your waiter to perform poorly, there's a very good chance that they also "tip out" to others, who actually did their job just fine, and deserve to be "punished" even less.

HOW TO BE A WAITER

Being a waiter has one basic thing in common with lots of other jobs, which is that you may end up doing it when you don't really want to be doing it. So if you ARE going to be one - whether you really want to or not - you may as well make the best of it, and maybe even try to *enjoy* it. But if the fact is that you absolutely HATE waiting tables and know you're worthy of better, go find it. Now. Because you're probably not the only one who's not enjoying your waiter experience. I can't believe how many people wait tables for the money, detest it, yet continue doing it. If you want to hate your job and make a lot of money, waste disposal, sewage work, and construction work all offer better compensation, and simpler interpersonal headaches. Honestly, if you really detest being a waiter, just stop. Your co-workers, your guests, and perhaps most importantly YOU will be much happier.

If you're somewhere in that middle ground of "I really don't love this but intend to make the best of it", it's probably helpful to ditch your ego a bit and ponder all the theatre references we've made so far. Acting skills come in very, very handy, so frankly, if you don't have *any* acting skills, you may still want to consider another source of income. At least being able to *act* like you don't hate your job is sort of a pre-requisite.

When I was a waiter, I had to summon every ounce of acting skills at my disposal. My appearance has led people to tell me I look like everyone from David Bowie to Max von Sydow to "that guy on that model show", so when I first walked up to the table people always had a hard time assessing whether I was the owner, a professional butler, or a down-on-his luck B-List celebrity. The net effect in any case was that I could never just walk up and wait a table in a normal fashion; people would either be offended that the owner didn't want to small-talk with them, or on the defensive about the idea that the arrogant waiter was going to embarrass them by having better etiquette than they do or something, and make it impossible for them to cram food in their yammering pie hole in the manner to which they were accustomed.

My main method for deflecting a lot of this projected hubris was to walk up and say "Hi there. How y'all doin' this evening". This strangely put everyone at ease by giving the impression that I was none of the things they expected, but instead a mild-mannered southern gentleman here to show them some hospitality. On the other hand, if I was waiting on large group of pompous *nouveau riche* twits who were completely ignoring my existence, I'd walk up and say in an extremely intimidating but well-modulated voice "Good Evening Everyone. May I Have Your Attention For A Moment", complete with the capital letters. I was blessed with a fairly authoritative voice, which serves one well waiting tables. With this kind of table, you have to take charge, as if you were Siegfried and Roy in the lion cage. If you have the chops to pull this off, the guests will treat you kindly and respectfully throughout the rest of the evening, entirely forgetting that they could in fact eat you alive or get you fired in a nanosecond.

In any case, as we've already pointed out, restaurants are indeed a bit like the theatre. The useful thing to remember here is that as a waiter, are not the star, the guests are. At least from their point of view. They're also the audience in a way, so "don't break the fourth wall". They don't want to hear the miserable details of your personal life, or really know what you think. You're definitely an important cast member, but it's a bit part. Know your role, and stick to it.

And dealing with the kitchen? Please, get a clue. Those people are trapped in a sweltering confined space working

FOR YOU for hours, while you prance around, jibber jabber, and probably sneak drinks all night from the bar.

Here is an unbelievably powerful tool for building bonds with the kitchen, a thing I can't believe more waitpeople never think of doing. It will change your work life forever. When business picks up, ask the kitchen crew if they want a soda or ice water, and make a beverage run for them. It will be received like you're Mother Freaking Theresa or something, and can be the start of an actually normal relationship with people that can otherwise make your life a living hell. Because face it - you're a jerk when your orders don't come out right. And they can really, really make your orders not come out right *on purpose*. Don't give them an incentive.

THE KITCHEN GUYS

THE CHEF

I long ago lost touch with what a "regular" person imagines a typical kitchen hierarchy to be like, but from talking to these "regular" people, I gather that they think there's some fellow back there wearing a Chef Boy Ardee hat and doing "mama mia kisses" on the tips of his fingers and saying "atsa spicy meata ball" when things turn out well.

So sorry to disappoint you. The vast majority of establishments don't have a chef, they have a head line cook of some kind, a generally valued, often hot-tempered, but in any case easily replaced person whose job is to lead the execution of an existing menu, with the support of a crew of underlings who may or may not have a variety of titles like "prep cook" or "sous chef" or "hot side" or "cold side". The many restaurants that don't have an actual chef probably *had* an actual chef involved at some point to create a menu, but this chef was either one of the owners (who probably isn't actually a "chef") or an executive or consultant chef, depending on the size of the organization.

When there IS a chef, there is an ego, and usually a passion. And they usually sport ball caps, not white paper tubes on their heads, and I've never actually seen one do the "perfecto finger kiss". So my advice for chefs everywhere? I dare offer none, because this would be like telling a rock star to stop demanding on their tour rider that their M&M's be sorted by color. That's the whole idea behind being a rock star or a chef - to be temperamental, demanding, and to throw temper tantrums when your peculiar needs aren't met! I jest of course. Because there are a lot of wonderful, patient, and level-headed chefs out there. But they tend to be self-motivated go-getters who march to their own drum. Let's just let them.

THE LINE

So in reality, that chef guy you probably imagine lording over the kitchen in his chef whites is often a grumpy, hung over, hard working guy with moderately poor social skills who really loves red meat, and in spite of his lack of finer culinary training, still exhibits all the worst temperamental traits of a "real" chef. At least that's the image that probably sticks in many waiters' heads. The truth is - at least in my experience - that there are about an equal number of line cooks that fit this stereotype as there are people who really enjoy the job, and do it calmly, happily and efficiently.

But if you ARE Chef Grumpypants, I have a LOT of advice for you. First, CHILL THE HELL OUT. We're all in this together. If standing in a sweltering box and watching an incessant stream of whiny waitstaff faces popping into a stainless-steel "food window" while you cook a dozen dishes at once stresses you out, consider another job. That's a hell of a set of tasks to pull off all at once. Don't feel badly if you can't cut it. And if your excuse for being a stress mess isn't the job itself, but the boss (a common sentiment), heed the words a crusty old prep cook shared with me years ago. This old German lady I worked with once said to me in a gravelly voice - while puffing on a Tareyton five feet from her prep area - "You always gonna hate you boss. I dono why people always bitchin' about they boss. You always gonna hate 'em. Get used to it."

Enough said. Much like the advice to waiters, if you don't like the blatantly obvious aspects of what your job really entails, GET A DIFFERENT ONE.

THE DISH GUY

I always laugh when wealthy white wingnut conservatives rant about getting all those darn foreigners out of the country so honest, God-fearing *Americans* can have those jobs they're stealing from us. Because about eighty percent of the jobs they're "stealing" are dishwashing jobs in restaurants nationwide. The industry would come screeching to a halt in a matter of weeks, as the country's restaurants quickly exhausted the first round of white suburban hires, who would all almost certainly quit in the first month.

But regardless of the uncomfortable realities of the racial and cultural demographics of dishwashing employees in America today, washing dishes in a restaurant - aside from being a grueling, repetitious, sweaty, mostly thankless job - is often also one of the lowest-paid positions. And ironically, one of the most crucial. Unless you'd like to start eating on paper plates and smelling the garbage as it piles up in the kitchen, 'cause the waitstaff sure as hell isn't touching that crap. If I could make it happen, dishwashers would be paid double the wage of anyone else in the building, share in the tips, and for their "e-meal", would get a take-home dinner for their family along with whatever they'd like for themselves.

Maybe I wrote the wrong book. Maybe it should have been *Why Everyone Should Wash Dishes for Two Weeks*.

SO WHY *SHOULD* EVERYONE WAIT
TABLES FOR TWO WEEKS?

So what have I been getting at with my somewhat pretentious and flimsily supported "History of Class Structure in America 101", these waiter anecdotes, and my unsolicited opinionating? If you yourself haven't waited tables for any period of time, you may be harboring a smug assumption that since misery loves company, the legions of us who already know the answer to the question "why should everyone wait tables for two weeks?" just want you to feel our pain briefly. Or perhaps - because of how the material has been presented - think that the *author* is the one who's being smug.

The fact is that restaurant work, and especially waiting tables, is hands-down the best all around intensive training to cultivate almost *any* workplace trait that is considered an asset. Waiting tables develops listening skills, presentation skills, thinking literally on one's feet, time/resource management skills, selling and teamwork skills, physical agility, hand/eye coordination, HR problem solving, and as an added bonus with all these other exceptional character builders, a decent waiter knows how to MOP. Which may seem like an irrelevant skill, until of course, something needs to be mopped. But mopping itself isn't the key here, it's merely a task that helps one *embrace the key*.

And that key is (here comes the "H" word again) *humility*.

If you're in any kind of leadership or management position, I have a fun idea for you to try with your new hires.

Want to see your young, smartphone-toting, Twitter-happy hipster employee turn into a deer in the headlights? Early in their training, at the end of the workday, say to them "Fantastic job today! You rock!" and then pull the mop and bucket out of the utility closet. After the initial look of perplexedness disappears, and they accept the fact that they're actually going to be asked to (gasp) MOP A FLOOR, the real comedy begins. No, the water has to be HOT. No, I mean reeeeeaaally HOT. WHOA! Not so much soap! The SOAP doesn't do the work, YOU do! No no no! Squeeze that sucker out before you start! We're CLEANING THE FLOOR, not WATERING THE GARDEN. By the time the person is done with this first terrifying mop experience, they're so eager to get back to just "doing their actual job" that it's like they spent six months in boot camp with Gunnery Sergeant Hartman in the movie *Full Metal Jacket*.

Anyone who has worked in restaurants knows this routine all too well. In foodservice, you have to spend entire workdays cleaning up people's drool, food scraps, and other dining and face-wiping debris, and then turn around and talk to them like you're their personal butler. It's like changing a baby's diaper and then having the baby say "good job, now go fetch my pipe and slippers, will you?" A simple task like mopping almost becomes therapeutic. This is probably why the military places such an emphasis on cleaning in basic training. Six months of mopping floors and cleaning toilets, and you'll do ANYTHING to move on to the next task, even if it's killing your fellow humans.

But the serious point I'm making here is that foodservice – specifically in a full service restaurant – gives a person a range of training that you will find in no other job, anywhere. If a person is doing it right, they're dealing with everything from sales and customer service, to maintaining product consistency, to ballet (try carrying a tray with six dinners on it through a crowded room!) to conflict resolution and therapy (as we pointed out, some kitchen lines are more like battlegrounds than work areas) to sanitation tasks like mopping and waste disposal.

Next time you're hiring some young green employees, don't just look at their education and the more "professional" school jobs they try to pad their resume with, look for a year at Mel's Diner.

So again, why *should* everyone wait tables for two weeks?

Well, the truth is that two weeks is probably not long enough.

SOME FINAL WORDS ON HUMILITY

It's something of a tragedy that our culture encourages the "anyone can be a millionaire" myth. For a few reasons. First of all, because it simply isn't true; very few people have the focus, financial savvy, and *determination* to become a millionaire. And second, because a million dollars just isn't that much money these days! But perhaps most importantly, because it encourages everyone to ACT like a millionaire, and encourages people who are merely financially "comfortable" - i.e.: not literally struggling from paycheck to paycheck - to treat people who *are* struggling in this way as their inferiors.

You see it every day in common interactions. People scolding grocery clerks, making insanely detailed customizations of their Starbucks order, dressing down dry cleaning clerks for a poorly creased garment, or generally treating fellow citizens as worthless peons who are merely IN THEIR WAY as they drive to work or walk down the street. But this tendency is nowhere more evident than in the dining room of even the most humble diner, where on top of being able to make one's royal demands, the guest (an interesting misnomer, in a way) also has the ability to determine the servant's wage on a whim!

And therein lies the cleverly cloaked gift that waiting tables presents one with; the trick is to realize that gift is there, and then embrace it with the calm determination required to nurture it. What is that gift?

Where else is one ever put in a situation where, while routinely being subjected to the most insidious of human behavior and egotistical whim, they are simultaneously required to maintain an exceptional level of dignity, humility, and acceptance of one's place in life, all while balancing six meals on a tray with one arm while *smiling*?

105

It's like trying to study with a Zen master while riding in a clown car at the circus! And to top it off, if you "fail", you get an instant pay cut. If one embraces these challenges successfully, they often come out of the experience with a character facet that can be achieved in almost no other way, save for volunteering with an overseas aid agency or something.

To be realistic about it, most people would probably not actually achieve this level of "enlightenment" while waiting tables, let alone survive the first shift. But the same lesson is available at any moment of your life; it's just a little more obfuscated. Although few situations in life provide the boot-camp-like training in this kind of character development the way waiting tables does, they still exist. Only a culture as cynical as ours could render the phrase "teachable moment" a naive cliché; they are in our face almost every moment of the day.

We tend to confuse the words "humility" and "humiliation". This is unfortunate, because while the latter is definitely something to be avoided, the former is perhaps one of the noblest and, coincidentally, most profitable character traits a person can develop. And this is not merely a warm and fuzzy notion about some airy-fairy high-minded spiritual concept; aside from all the anecdotal references to the value of humility by great leaders and thinkers throughout history, and the academic studies that validate the truism that humility is a leadership trait, there was an interesting recent example from the business world, where humility was the *last* thing that was expected to be a factor in success.

Business consultant Jim Collins spent five years studying what makes "great" companies great. "Great" companies were defined as those whose "financial performance exceeded the market average by several orders of magnitude over a sustained period of time". A key characteristic of the leaders of those companies? Humility as a primary personality trait.

As C.S. Lewis said, "Humility is not thinking less of yourself, it's thinking of yourself less."

DESSERT

You know that feeling, right after eating a huge meal, of "Oh my God I want to die why did I eat so much"? That diabetic coma that makes you feel exhausted, maybe even gives you a dull physical pain all over? It's a poorly understood fact that dessert will often alleviate this miserable state, by providing a much-needed sugar boost. A benefit that will be even further enhanced by enjoying that sugar with a healthy blast of caffeine.

It's a bit ironic that many people will sit down to a four-thousand-calorie meal, loaded with meat proteins, insane amounts of fats and oils, and more carbohydrates than a marathon runner needs for the first leg of a marathon, and then reach the end, and sheepishly say "I couldn't possibly! I'd feel like such a pig!"

Their loss, because those in the know get to eat their vulgar feast AND enjoy some sweets after. And that's what the next section is about. We know that most people who would give a book about waiting tables even a passing glance are secretly looking for a *Kitchen Confidential* style exposé that verifies all the terrible things they *want* to believe about what goes on behind the scenes in a restaurant.

This section is for you. While we won't be delving into labored descriptions of doing cocaine on the cutting board or putting horrifying things in your hollandaise sauce at brunch, we will not only share some amusing anecdotes, we'll offer some "guest training" that may help you avoid being "that customer" when you dine out. Because trust me, you do not want to be *that customer*.

On the other hand, if you're someone who has worked in the industry, the next section is meant as a bit of a prod. There's a good chance that as you read the few war stories shared, you'll say "PUH! That story is a damn FAIRY TALE compared to some of the things I've seen go down!" If that's the case, we hope you'll visit the website for the book, and share your own story there.

For now though, let's see what's on the dessert tray.

DINING OUT ON HOLIDAYS

Those who have at one time or another worked in the industry will be well aware of the "other side" of dining out on holidays, but if you are not now and have never been a member of this fine community, it might benefit you to ponder these ideas the next time you plan on avoiding the challenges of actually entertaining guests *yourself* on holidays, the way your grandma and grandpa did. The patchy service and frazzled staff when you dine out on holidays are usually not due to ineptitude or contempt; more often, it's the overall sickening dynamic created by the *guests* that is responsible.

VALENTINE'S DAY

If you've ever been on a first date on Valentine's Day, or know the vague unease of taking your relatively new boyfriend or girlfriend on the first Valentine's Day date of the relationship, you have experienced one tenth of the tense terror, and even less of the immense rage that can accompany waiting tables on this sadistically demented holiday.

It took me a few years of my early table waiting career to understand why this holiday - no matter how positively you approached it - would always turn out to be such a tense - and sometimes almost surreal - evening. So let me walk you through it.

112

First, take an entire restaurant that is usually comprised of a variety of tables that seat anywhere from 2 to 20 people, and set the whole place up so that all the tables are optimized for seating two. Second, take a chef who probably hasn't had a healthy relationship in years because of his long hours and the fact that he always comes home smelling of garlic, seared meat, and sweat, and force him to dream up a custom menu meant to be feasted on by starry-eyed lovers whose faces he will never see.

Then, take the otherwise generic dining room and put white linens, candles, and roses everywhere. Don't forget to run specials on splits of champagne. This is probably thrown in for comic relief. If you've ever seen a typical inept waiter bumble with a bottle of bubbly, the effect is even more comical when they try to go through the same motions with a toy-sized version.

So far this probably doesn't sound so bad, right? But now look at a couple of factors from the service point of view. It is - contrary to what you might think - immensely harder to wait on four two-tops than one eight-top or two four tops. And we have just turned an entire restaurant into two tops. And serving a custom menu places another level of strain on both the servers and the kitchen staff. Especially when all the dishes are cooked two-by-two like Noah loading animals onto the Ark.

But those minor logistical issues are trivial compared to what the *real* horror of what this holiday is all about, which is the gut wrenching tension in the air caused by the guests. Think about it. Every person insane or ignorant enough to dine out on this holiday is not only an insecure amateur diner with a chip on their shoulder about the high prices and their own feeble dining knowledge and skills, they're also either a.) Trying to impress a relative stranger, or - and this can be even worse - b.) Trying to please a spouse or long-term partner.

The atmosphere in many restaurants on Valentine's Day can be a PTSD-inducing trauma for the staff, as they meander this minefield trying to pacify the combatants on the battlefield of love as they stage this unintentional insurgency. The air is thick with the tension of dozens of people (guests and staff alike) all fretting about pleasing someone else, a someone else who will probably not be pleased because of their skewed expectations.

I honestly don't remember a single Valentine's Day where someone didn't end up crying, more often because they didn't know how to respond to the wedding proposal lobbed in from left field than out of joy. Unless you take a perverse joy in Schadenfreude, there is nothing sadder than the sight of a well-dressed woman running from a restaurant sobbing, except for the sight of the shell-shocked guy left sitting there with a diamond ring that probably just depreciated 40% upon purchasing it. At least he'll generate a good bar tab if he sticks around.

So my advice for Valentine's Day dining? Learn to cook.

Mother's Day

Given that your restaurant critiquing skills so far in life have been confined to short-tipping the waitress at Appleby's because she was too slow bringing ranch dip refills for your potato skins, don't start acting like you know how to dine at this level NOW. No-one's gonna fall for it. Not the waiter, not the owner, and especially not your mom. Having meltdowns about the inevitably bad service being provided by the server that's overwhelmed with amateur numbnuts like yourself will create the only experience that could be worse than if you tried cooking dinner yourself.

THANKSGIVING & CHRISTMAS

These two holidays have one important thing in common that highlights what kind of person would dine out on them. They are both holidays where a key element is the joy of preparing food with your loved ones. Yes, we know you love your bartender, but do you love your waiter? Your busser? The kitchen staff that works their asses off more than forty hours every week preparing food for total strangers, so they can keep food on the table for the ones THEY love? Who by the way are eating without them today. Or maybe not eating at all, because maybe they do all the cooking for the family too. Good job, *Grinch Who Stole Christmas*. You are single-handedly contributing to the demise of the American Family, just so you don't have to eat turkey TV dinners again this year.

A special exception here is of course allowed for Jewish people going to Chinese restaurants on these days.

NEW YEAR'S EVE

Okay, it's New Year's Eve, and you're sitting at a high-priced restaurant. Maybe with one person, maybe with a group. Put down that damn duck call you've been blowing into periodically for the last hour or two, and look around. Of all the dozens or even hundreds of people around you, how many of them look GENUINELY happy? Certainly not the waitstaff and bartenders; that's kind of a given. But honestly, given the choice of a quiet evening at home or a wild party at your or a friend's house, where you can move around, mingle, not worry about getting cut off, and where there are probably many more bushes to "toss your cookies" into later, why, oh why in the name of God would you make reservations that cost hundreds, perhaps THOUSANDS of dollars at a restaurant on New Year's Eve? I don't even wait tables anymore, but I hope you get arrested on the way home tonight, after throwing up on the cop's shoes while he's asking for your driver's license.

BIRTHDAYS

One of the bosses early in my career was of the meat-cleaver-wielding variety that I mentioned in the "How to Be" section. But accenting his management-by-intimidation manner was a wicked sense of humor, which would make unexpected appearances while engaging in the most mundane tasks.

He was always gleeful to be the one answering the phone when someone called to ask if we did anything special for birthdays. He thought the idea of birthday specials was moronic, based on the two simple facts that 1.) You are really not that special, and 2.) People are born every day of the year, so you may as well just give away a few free entrees every day if you're going to do silly things like buy one, get one free birthday specials. So when a customer called to ask about them, he would graciously apologize, saying "No, I'm terribly sorry, we don't do birthday specials. But I hear there's a shoe store at the mall that gives away a free pair of shoes on your birthday." People being the self-obsessed twits they are, they would almost always excitedly ask which store, and he would politely reply that he didn't know, and that maybe they should call the mall.

To this day, I wonder how many times people working at malls wondered who the hell it was out there who was feeding people this line. But the bottom line is that if you're twelve or under, more power to you if you want a restaurant to do something special on your birthday. But if you're not, give up on the idea that the staff owes it to you to surround your table and clap in unison singing "I don't know but I been told! Someone here is gettin' old!" in a military cadence.

STAGE MANAGEMENT

The interesting thing about the meat-cleaver-wielding owner that I mentioned in that last story is the fact is that he never - at least to the best of my knowledge - actually wielded a meat cleaver at anyone. But he *did* do a good job of giving the *impression* that he would wield a meat cleaver if a situation demanded it. He was actually quite a genius; when he wasn't busy terrorizing the staff of the restaurant, he was usually working on some kind of engineering project. One of these projects was patenting that pasta machine we mentioned earlier. This was way back in the early 70's, before most Americans knew there WAS such a thing as fresh pasta. Always ahead of the curve, around the same time he opened that sushi bar we mentioned, which was probably the first sushi bar in the Midwest, and just to keep people (the waitstaff mostly) on their toes, he opened a gay nightclub. It was at the restaurant for which he had designed the pasta machine that I had my first encounter with him.

It was my first night on the job, and I was just a little bit nervous; I had only trained for two shifts, and I was bartending on a "football Saturday". The small college town I lived in had one of the winningest college teams in the country, and a stadium that seated over 100,000 people. On game days, the town was gridlocked with game traffic, and restaurants were often booked beyond capacity for the entire evening.

It was a few minutes before opening time, and although we had been sneaking out the side door to keep tabs on the immense line forming out front, the staff was calm and collected; except for me, they had all worked at this place for several years and had their routines down. It was at this point - about ten minutes before opening - that the owner came down from the office, and announced he had something to say. Putting it that way doesn't convey the vibe of what he actually did; his presence alone always sort of brought everyone to attention, and what he actually said was something like "I want to talk to you fucking idiots. Everyone come here."

He then planted himself with his back to me, one elbow on the bar, facing the staff. He used his other arm to gesture with a huge stack of guest checks as he began yelling. "You see these checks from last night?" he began. "I went through three hundred of these fucking things, and you know what I found? THREE COFFEES! Are you fucking kidding me? Are you people trying to fucking tell me that with over five hundred fucking people eating here last night, you only sold THREE GODDAMN COFFEES?"

As he continued to yell at them about tracking sales and how if they DID only sell three coffees, they were idiots, and how if they *had* simply forgotten to write them on the checks, he had lost several hundred dollars. Somewhere in the yelling and gesticulating, he hurled the entire stack of guest checks (the card stock kind, not the flimsy paper kind) into the dining room as punctuation. He must have practiced this move at home or something; it was impressive how thoroughly the checks seemed to disperse to every corner of the small restaurant.

It was now about five minutes before opening, and one of this fellow's other pet peeves was not opening on time, so the staff was running around like little monkeys rounding up guest checks, and suddenly scrambling to make sure they hadn't forgotten any little setup details. This whole time I was glad that I had basically been staring at his back as he yelled at everyone else; I had nothing to do with what he was yelling about, and wasn't especially in the mood to get screamed at on one of my first nights on the job.

Not quite finished with his tirade, he continued yelling about all sorts of things, like how he treated the staff like family and how they robbed him blind every day, that sort of thing. As he continued his seemingly insane rant and the clock ticked closer to opening time, he moved on to a particularly dramatic speech about what it would be like filing for bankruptcy because of all the coffee that the staff had failed to charge for, which he estimated was costing him over forty thousand dollars a year.

It was as he was reaching the climax of this particular passage, as he yelled - with the periods nearly visible in the air - "FORTY. THOUSAND. FUCKING. DOLLARS", that he turned to me, and said - in the calmest, sweetest, most paternal voice ever, made even more charming by his Turkish accent, "Could you get me an orange juice please baby?" And then turned around and continued yelling.

He finished his rant immediately after that, set the empty orange juice glass on the bar, calmly put his hand on mine and said "thank you. I really needed that", and then stormed out of the restaurant and back up the stairs to the office. The staff of course was now completely tweaked into a frenzy, muttering about what an ass the owner was as they hustled to make sure things were in order as the mass of customers flowed in the front door.

Now you could take this in as just another amusing restaurant story, thinking "Yup, another nutty ethnic restaurant owner". But that would be missing the point completely. This was really something much more interesting, and it was calculated. Have you ever worked in theatre? Do you know what kind of shenanigans a stage manager may have to engage in to do a good job? Keeping a cast or ensemble on the "right edge" can be one of the most powerful tools in their arsenal. A well-rehearsed cast or dance company can become incredibly lackadaisical in their pre-showtime demeanor, especially if the show has been playing for a few weeks. It's not uncommon for a stage manager to "play" them, feeding them vague disinformation about how full the house is or changing up the five minute calls, merely to keep them "alive" to help avoid a flat opening.

After I had worked for this fellow for a couple of years, I asked him if that's what he was doing in scenarios like this, and after sharing that yes, this and other tricks were part of a carefully thought-out management method, he looked at me and said "I guess you're not as fucking stupid as you look". Which I knew meant, "You're alright. In fact you're one of my best people." Because if he had meant anything else, he would have responded to my question with "Will you shut the fuck up, stop asking stupid questions, and fetch me an espresso?"

AN ACCIDENTAL TRIP TO CHINA

Well, not an *actual* trip to China. But for three years I found myself immersed in Chinese-American culture, as I basically stumbled into a job managing a Chinese restaurant. And during this time I learned a tremendous amount about American management methods, by working with the *absence* of them. This experience led to some of the funniest restaurant experiences I had in my couple of decades of on and off restaurant work, one of which I'll get to shortly.

It all began when I hired in as a weekend bartender for what - at the time - was a very ahead-of-the-curve Chinese restaurant. In an era when the majority of Chinese places were still serving Egg Foo Yung and Chop Suey, this place served a much finer menu based on dishes that had been refined in Hong Kong, Taipei, and New York restaurants. After working at the place for a couple of months, the out-of-town Taiwanese owner - who stopped in periodically for a few days to keep an eye on things - asked me if I'd be interested in managing the place. I joked about what an interesting twist that would be; to the best of my knowledge it would make me the only pale blonde Chinese restaurant manager in the state.

He explained that although he had enjoyed solid dominance of the local market for a few years, mainly because his menu simply blew all the "old school" Chinese places out of the water, he had seen his sales slip a bit as a couple of similar places had opened. He figured that one thing that would give him a genuine competitive edge was decent service. To this day, it is probably fairly common that some of the "worst service" one might experience will be in an Asian restaurant. To be fair, it's not necessarily always "bad" service, often it's just "different" than what a Euro-American, western guest might desire.

127

In any case, the owner had noticed that when the restaurant got busy, I would reflexively jump in to help in the dining room if the bar wasn't busy, which he pointed out kind of freaked out the staff, because they couldn't believe I wasn't asking for a tipout, and therefore figured I had some other agenda, like stealing their tips, or maybe *buying* the place. They honestly couldn't suss it out, and that's what gave him the idea to make me manager; he knew it would throw them off and make them tread carefully.

I could probably write an entire training manual based on what I learned from this job, but one of the more simple and enlightening things was this: Chinese culture has a quiet deep wisdom that can easily come across as laziness or apathy. I learned part of this lesson at the first employee meeting I scheduled. I figured that given their general experience with managers being family members or personal favorites of the owner, who managed with a sort of unilateral "I'm the boss and what I say goes" kind of style, that the staff would find it refreshing and motivating to be able to have input.

"EEEENNNH!" [Insert game show "WRONG ANSWER" sound effect here.]

One of the first amusing things about this new position was that the staff generally had a hard time pronouncing my name, with its long "e" followed by a "y" as consonant. It pretty quickly became the single syllable "e", which, as one of the waiters pointed out, was pretty handy, since it sounded like "yi", the Chinese word for the number one.

So as the new, Caucasian, "number one" in the establishment, I had taken it upon myself to do something unheard of, i.e.: have a staff meeting. I kept

128

my introduction brief, and mostly explained - as the owner sat nearby to lend authority - that my only goal was to help improve service and sales, and that I would only make changes after working side by side with the staff for a month or so. Their eyes widened a bit when I said I was going to spend a few days on every job in the restaurant, including dishwasher and line cook; they had never seen a manager do such a thing.

I really thought I had them at this point, that they'd be thinking, "oh man, maybe this guy is for REAL". So I then wrapped things up by saying that I really valued any insights, suggestions, or even complaints before we finished the meeting. I was really surprised by the response, which was...DEAD. SILENCE. "No really! Anybody? Surely you have SOMETHING to say!" Stone faces and more silence. "Anyone? Bueller?" More silence and stony faces. I asked the owner immediately after the "meeting" what had just happened, and he said:

"They're just smart. They know that the less they talk the sooner the meeting will be over"

As I said, this job taught me things I would never learn in any conventional American setting. Things like why communism may in fact actually suck, just like we were brainwashed to believe as the gun-toting, flag waving, pinko haters we mostly are. The owner once pointed out – as I was trying to sort out who the lazy employees were and why – that mostly the lazy ones were from mainland China, because they had grown up in a world where no matter how hard you did or didn't work, you'd get paid the same amount and probably never get promoted. This led to an hilarious conversation about how to get the staff to take phone messages instead of mechanically saying "Okay I tell him bye" and going back to staring into space like they had been before they were so rudely interrupted. He said he had thought about paying them a quarter a message, but figured then they'd be breaking each other's arms elbowing their way to answer the phone, or making up messages just to pad their income.

As we discussed various theories of income-based incentives, the conversation meandered a bit, and he shared an idea that I think we could all agree with; I may someday form a lobby group and try to get it passed as a law.

He said that he had always thought that doctors should start out with a really, really high wage, and have it reduced every time they lost a patient.

MAYBE TIPPING *IS* A CITY IN CHINA

Tipping. As far as a lot of Asian restaurant waitstaff are concerned it *may as well* be a city in China, as the old joke goes. To this day, with the exception of hipper, urban Asian restaurants that are not family owned and operated, the way the little game of tipping plays out explains a lot about human nature.

At this place I managed, the compensation model was all over the map. I was paid a fixed salary, but often got HUGE bonuses quarterly. I say "often", because there was rarely any explanation of why one quarter I'd get a couple hundred bucks, and another a couple THOUSAND. The kitchen staff made anywhere from $40K a year, on down to near-slave wages that were balanced out with free housing and food.

Most of the wait staff were paid fifteen dollars a day plus tips. You read that right. It was the late twentieth century, and employees somewhere in America were still being paid about a dollar an hour. On the other hand, the place was open for twelve hours straight every day, and there was no formal "break schedule". Which may sound like more labor exploitation, but frankly, it's hard to tell "gossiping while cleaning snow peas" from "taking a break", so it tended to balance out. And for staff that bothered to show even the slightest indication of motivation beyond the task of merely delivering food and waiting until guests left the restaurant to finally return to clear their debris-covered table, there were hefty bonuses from the owner, which inevitably would be slyly mentioned to co-workers at the "snow pea table".

This unfortunately had the opposite of the intended effect. Instead of seeing someone else making more money and emulating how they did so, the other staff would become even *more* bitter, and give even *worse* service. Which demonstrates the phenomenon I at the time referred to with the owner as the "Negative Growth Gratuity Recursion" (he was a scientist in his other work, and we often made up joke technical names).

If you've ever experienced crappy service in a Chinese restaurant and left a crappy tip as a result, this death spiral of bad service and bad compensation is probably as much YOUR fault as the server's. You see, it's nearly impossible to break the "I'm not gonna give them good service they tip crappy" cycle, because once it is in motion, it becomes a mutual expectation. It took us over two years to really break down this vicious cycle, partly because no matter how well we trained new staff and made progress with the older staff, we really needed to wait for some of the jaded senior staff to turn over for the attitude to take hold. It's a fact that any experienced restaurant worker is well aware of – no matter *what* cuisine they're serving – that the real power in a restaurant is often in the hands of some crusty old hanger-on employee, not the manager.

But at the end of the day, the real problem lay with the customer. It didn't matter how much we improved service, because there's a particular type of customer in America who is drawn to Chinese restaurants precisely because of this "tradition". We have a technical term for them. It's "STIFF".

BRO JOBS & THUAT

I could share more about the peculiarities of being a white guy managing a Chinese restaurant; in fact I'm working on a long-term project compiling how "old world" business methods impact modern American businesses. But I'll leave you with one of the more amusing of the dozens of hilarious stories about things that happened during my three year stint at this restaurant.

First of all, it's probably relevant somehow to describe the decor of the joint, and its history. In the sixties, long before it became a Chinese restaurant, the fellow who opened it had gone to Los Angeles and seen a "Googie" era diner that had a huge eyeball as the main design element of its wacky early sixties sign. Upon returning to town (a small Midwestern college town, for the record), he decided he wanted to replicate the idea, and set about building a Tiki-themed restaurant/nightclub, with a cave-like organic ceiling and walls. Even thirty years later, it literally looked like the Flintstone's house inside, because the stuff used for the walls was harder than any concrete known to man, was still fully intact, and was not going away any time soon. I mean, they must have used alien technology to create the stuff, because whenever we needed to drill into it, it would break diamond drill bits like they were rock candy.

From the outside, the placed looked like a nineteenth century submarine or something. The original owner's dream of a bright shiny eyeball scanning the horizon for dinner guests was immediately dashed by the other local merchants at the time, who weren't about to let this nut disrupt their otherwise droll and functional sixties business strip. Blinking neon and a Norge Cleaner Sputnik-like sign – both familiar sites nearby – were where they drew the line. No eyeballs next to MY strip mall, thank you very much. As a result, the tower

137

originally built to support the eye vaguely resembled the conning tower of a submarine. On the bright side, the owner still got to install a waterfall inside the tower as he had originally intended, and the place was christened "Kale's Waterfall".

But I digress. I merely wanted to set the stage so that the surreality of the evening in question would be complete. This was before I was promoted to managing the full restaurant; I'd been managing the bar for a few months at this point, and had made a point of hiring and training a hip and attractive crew of bartenders. As a result, the formerly creepy and abandoned cocktail lounge was packed on weekend nights, partly from the new regulars who liked the crowd and simply came for drinks, and partly from the parties waiting to get seated for dinner.

So one Friday, a couple sat at the bar and ordered what was at the time - it was the late 80's - a fairly common nightclub drink called a "blowjob". There were many variations of exactly which syrupy liqueurs were in the drink, but it usually was topped with whipped cream. The couple thought they were being clever and naughty, and we as seasoned bartenders thought they were being twits, but played along, making jokes about all the other stupid nightclub drinks like the "Sex on the Beach", the "Fuzzy Navel" and the "Screaming Orgasm".

A little while later the couple got seated in the dining room, and the bar got even more packed. There are really few things weirder than being the only white employee slinging drinks in a Chinese restaurant bar that looks more like the "Bedrock Bar and Grille", but we were having fun, in spite of the slightly raucous crowd and MTV blaring on the television. In the middle of this hustle and bustle, one of the Vietnamese waitresses approached the service bar to order drinks, and yelled:

"Ian, I have customer who needs blow job!"

The bar of course went dead silent, except for the MC Hammer blaring on the television.

All eyes at this moment naturally fixed on me, and I didn't miss a beat, saying:

"Well Lien, I'm sorry, but that's just not in my job description".

The bar of course busted up laughing, and things returned to business as usual pretty quickly, except that we then of course had to make about a half-dozen rounds of "Blow Jobs", and spend the next half hour talking about stupid sex-themed nightclub drinks.

The poor waitress knew that something awkward had happened, but in spite of her pleas, it was another several months before we managed to get someone to translate and explain to her what had happened. That someone, in an ironic twist, was her brother, whose name was Thuat. And I'm sorry to report that the "thu" in his name was pronounced like a "tw".

THE TIPPING POINT

As this book goes to press, there is a raging debate in the food industry that could undermine the entire foundation of the concept this book is built upon. The debate is about one of the most defining aspects of waiting tables, i.e.: tipping. The arguments on both sides of the debate ironically rely on the same simple truth as the rationale behind their argument, but reach polar conclusions. Proponents of tipping lay bare the classist overtones of tipping when defending the practice, and arguing against building the tip into the cost of the meal somehow. A *Chicago Tribune* editorial of September 2013 put it this way:

> "From a customer's perspective, a predetermined tip is mighty presumptuous, a server who doesn't have to earn his or her tips has little incentive to try, and the customer has no choice but to pay a premium anyway."

The argument from the other side points out that tipping is a smug power play, one that is rooted in an archaic nineteenth century practice. The thrust of the argument against tipping is that it is based on the classism of European elites who forced the practice on hapless American service workers to establish their dominance over them. As a *New York Times* reader in 1899 put it:

> "I consider it degrading to the giver as well as to the receiver. The very shamefacedness with which it is practiced stamps it with the feature of blackmail and bribery. And the thralldom and yoke under which it puts its victim is truly sad to behold."

Perhaps a bit dramatically stated, but it was after all the nineteenth century.

Having worked in the industry for years myself, I certainly have *my* opinions on the topic, which I'll get to shortly. But I have to confess I'm astounded by the views of some of the people I know who are still in the industry today. Quite a few of them - whether they are servers of some kind, or owners - are lighting their torches and sharpening their pitchforks in preparation for some mass labor strike or something. Their argument is not far removed from that of the nineteenth century New York Times reader's, asserting that it is an abusive, arbitrarily implemented tool of the arrogant robber barons who until recently were more often referred to as "guests". They say it creates an unfair and demeaning wage structure, and that it must be abolished in order for any sane self-respecting person to survive in the ruthless sweatshops we more often refer to as "restaurants". They also suggest that eliminating tipping will improve service, and create more palatable, predictable pricing for the robber barons we just referenced.

I personally can't imagine more wrong-headed thinking.

My personal opinion is that although this debate does indeed have its roots in classism and issues of subservience between human beings, that is exactly the beauty of the practice! I can't help thinking that anyone who waits tables and would prefer tipping be abolished is probably just horrible at their job. Even in the cheapest of restaurants, a waitperson can easily make upwards of twenty bucks an hour. When I worked in fine dining, my base requirement was that I make thirty-five or more. If the establishment staffed and scheduled in a way that made this impossible, I'd look for a new job. And somewhat counterintuitively, when I DID happen to work in casual diner-like joints, the hourly wage could be even *higher*. Granted, you'd have to hustle more for that income, but the shifts would be short and the time usually flew by.

Do you enjoy eating at Panera, Chipotle, or McDonalds? Because that is the kind of experience you're likely to get if the American foodservice industry makes the paradigm shift to fixed wage income for waitpeople. Unless of course they make that fixed wage thirty bucks or more an hour and price your dinner accordingly to stay in business, which few restaurant owners could get away with, or *want* to get away with.

While restaurant work is a perfectly respectable career choice, most career people have chosen a lifestyle that they can afford that matches the wages they are able to generate. Far more people working in the industry are waiting tables as a temporary source of income on their way to something else. And yes, there are plenty of people in the industry who genuinely need a higher income and struggle to live on their server wages, but this is true with *any* industry. A person's failure to secure the appropriate career and income that comes with it is a personal problem, and a broader cultural problem. Tip income is hardly the CAUSE of these problems, it's merely a potential "symptom", if one is going to posit it as problem at all.

The horrible and inhuman game of master and servant that the anti-tip movement is so up in arms about is like so many other pet grievances in modern life. Some ideal of perfect equality is held up as the standard for all of humanity, when we all know darn well that we aren't all equal.

But even if we *were* equal, embracing the concept of service to others is one of the greatest gifts that life has to offer.

And when waiting tables, you actually get paid to do it!

THE TAKEOUT BOX

This Coffee Break Edition of *Why Everyone Should Wait Tables for Two Weeks* is intentionally a little light on "war stories"; an expanded edition is in the works which will include an entire section of not only my stories but those contributed by others. If you ever did a stint in foodservice and have a great story, visit:

WhyEveryoneShouldWaitTablesForTwoWeeks.com

And learn how to submit yours. You can also use that site to tell me how wrongheaded my thoughts on tipping are, apologize for the crappy tip you left me years ago, or explain why I *deserved* that crappy tip.

These remaining pages are merely an appendix of sorts, containing some random thoughts and anecdotes that didn't really fit elsewhere. We intend to expand this section quite a bit in the expanded edition, hopefully with YOUR stories.

ENGINEERED CO-WORKER INSULTS

Years ago I worked with a seasoned waiter who walked up to me on my first day on the job and said "Look Ian, I've been a waiter for a really long time, and at the age of forty I really, REALLY don't like my job. As a result, I have a lot of hostility that I obviously can't take out on the customers, so we've developed a little tradition here at the Oyster Bar. As the bartender, you're sort of trapped here, and as the waiter I'm going to have to walk up and ask you for something every few minutes, all night long. I've found it very effective to exchange ethnic, hereditary, social, religious and political stances with the new hires, so that throughout the evening we can exchange more articulate insults and barbs with each other. We're inevitably going to do it anyway, and I find the added accuracy makes it that much more rewarding."

I'll Take 'em. I Hate ALL my customers.

Toward the end of my waiting career, I ended up with a sort of cynical sense of equality. One in which, when all my co-workers were refusing to take the incredibly annoying regular, I'd say, "I'll take them, I hate ALL my customers". Something I really meant. Embedding the humor in the interaction made my basic unhappiness with my job much more bearable.

Finishing Sentences...

...in your head. If you're having a particularly bad day serving guests, one odd habit that I found helpful while serving people was to finish certain sentences in my head. For example, when you greet a table, out loud you say "How is everyone this evening?", but in your head, you finish with "I mean, besides ignorant, classless and obese?" Or when an obnoxious customer barks some inane command at you, out loud you say "Certainly sir", while in your head you say "right after I jam this salad fork down your throat". I found this to be surprisingly effective, you just have to be careful not to say these things out loud when you get really busy and distracted. And it can be hard to shut off when the shift is over.

Conditioned Nod Response Abuse

One of the most childish and interculturally hostile things I ever did while waiting tables was something I would do occasionally to amuse a co-worker, usually when I was hung over and irritated about having to serve others. If I was given a table of Japanese businessmen (which was fairly common in the towns where I did most of my restaurant work) I'd tell my co-worker to watch as I made them nod unnecessarily a half dozen times by nodding at irregular points while serving them. It worked with surprising consistency, but what it mostly "worked" at was proving that I was a jerk who shouldn't be waiting tables.

EARWORMS FOR DINNER

If you have a significant amount of experience waiting tables, you may already be familiar with this cruel game. It's inevitable that once in a while, in the midst of a hectic shift, some annoying song will get stuck in your head. For amusement, get proactive about this strange unconscious function of the human brain, and start humming tunes *on purpose* to terrorize your co-workers. Some especially effective songs are also the most irritating. Try tunes like *The Pina Colada Song* or *We Built This City*.

FARTING AT THE TABLE

Have you ever been out to dinner, suddenly detected an unpleasant odor, and wondered in horror which of your fellow diners had committed such an atrocity? Well ponder this: maybe it was the waiter, and maybe he did it *on purpose*. I once worked with a fellow who would actually say "Hey Ian, watch this. I'm going to go fart at the table." And then walk over to the table and start describing the specials while discreetly breaking wind. Consistently, one or two of the guests would wrinkle their nose subtly, and look around suspiciously at their fellow diners. Because surely, the waiter wouldn't just stand there and fart while describing the specials, RIGHT?

THIS IS A NIGHTCLUB, NOT A CIRCUS, OKAY?

These words were actually shouted at me by a manager one night in the "Tom Cruise in Cocktail" style nightclub I was working in, shortly after an incident involving a combination of breathing fire and demonstrating how you can swing a loaded cocktail tray in a 360-degree circle without spilling a drop. We'll share the details in the expanded edition, but for now, thanks for joining us this evening, and remember, we'd love for you to share your story at:

WhyEveryoneShouldWaitTablesForTwoWeeks.com

THE ELEVEN COMMANDMENTS

IAN GRAY

These were on the bulletin board of the break room in a restaurant where I spent a couple of years as a bartender and waiter. I crafted them with a co-worker named - no joke - *Moses*.

COMMANDMENTS FOR WAITERS

Although thou art called waiter, thou shalt not keep the guest waiting unnecessarily.

Thou shalt not introduce thyself without being asked, unless thou art employed by Applebees.

When thou art serving entrees, thou shalt not ask who ordered what.

Under penalty of death by stoning, though shalt not utter the phrase "is everything GREAT tonight?"

Though shalt not pull the old "double tip trick" on large parties.

COMMANDMENTS FOR GUESTS

Thou shalt not rudely demand to know "what's your name hun?" or "what's your name son?"

Thou shalt not pointlessly double-trip and triple-trip the server with trivial needs.

Thou shalt not request ketchup for thy Tournedos Forrestier. Just kidding. It's your steak, wreck it.

Thou shalt not apply mysterious demerit systems to tipping. If there is a problem, address it with management, not arbitrary punitive wage practices.

WHY WAIT

Thou shalt not order Ahi cooked well, Lamb Chops cooked rare, nor coffee that is half decalf and half regular.

Thou shalt not drink the fingerbowl. On second thought, go ahead. It's pretty funny when you do.

Made in the USA
San Bernardino, CA
29 August 2017